# PUNCHEONS & FLAGONS

## The Official Dungeons & Dragons Cocktail Book

Andrew Wheeler

Recipes by Ashley Stoyanov

Photographs by Ray Kachatorian

TEN SPEED PRESS
California | New York

WIZARDS
OF THE COAST
OFFICIAL LICENSED PRODUCT

# CONTENTS

One-Eyed Jax

The Gilded Horseshoe Inn

The Driftwood Tavern

The Moonstone Mask

The Pink Flumph

The Yawning Portal

The Halfway Inn

The Low Lantern

The Hissing Stones

The Hearth

Sea of Swords

The North

Anauroch

The Heartlands

Amn

Lantan

Tethyr

# INTRODUCTION

Adventures often begin in taverns. It's where parties meet, where travelers seek refuge, where bards sing and brawlers fight, where thieves make away with coin from an unsuspecting mark, and where rival wizards and warlocks break bread on neutral ground.

On every continent, in every world, on every plane of existence, there is always a tavern—or something very like one. One might wonder if taverns are more commonplace in Dungeons & Dragons than dungeons. Or dragons.

While taverns are universal, they are not all the same. The infamous Yawning Portal in Waterdeep is the archetypal adventurer's tavern with its rowdy patrons, beer-soaked boards, and direct connection to possible quests via the giant well that leads right to the dangerous treasure-filled dungeons of the Undermountain! Other venues are distinctly different: the Driftwood Tavern is a historic public house, the Pink Flumph is a raucous downtown theater, the Halfway Inn is a lonely trading post on a long road, the Moonstone Mask is a genteel club, and the Hissing Stones is a restful thermal spa.

In the following pages, you will encounter these places from all across the continent of Faerûn in the Forgotten Realms. You'll discover what sets each venue apart in terms of ambience, character, and clientele. You'll find recipes for popular, distinctive cocktails and appetizers that are the specialty of each house, and you'll learn a little something about the stories attached to those drinks and bites.

An adventurer's tavern is not just mead and wine and salty songs. The drinks on offer can be as diverse, colorful, and strange as the members of your adventuring party.

Welcome to the puncheons and flagons of Faerûn!

# ABOUT THIS BOOK

When we made these recipes, we hoped they would be used by Dungeons & Dragons players in social settings, perhaps even at the gaming table. All recipes are therefore designed to serve at least two people, and many of the drinks are punches—or rather, puncheons—that are perfect for sharing with an entire adventuring party.

*Puncheons & Flagons* is divided into ten chapters, and each chapter corresponds to one establishment in Faerûn and one base spirit or category of drinks. The first six chapters cover gin, whiskey, vodka, rum, tequila, and brandy. The subsequent chapters cover less ubiquitous spirits; wine-based drinks; beer, cider, and mead-based drinks; and alcohol-free drinks. Each chapter also includes a recipe for a shareable snack, something sweet or savory that pairs well with the drinks in that chapter and the atmosphere of that establishment.

Several of the recipes in this book require advance preparation and a little time in the kitchen, so always be sure to read the recipe from start to finish to see if you need to prepare a flavored syrup or make a miso-washed rum!

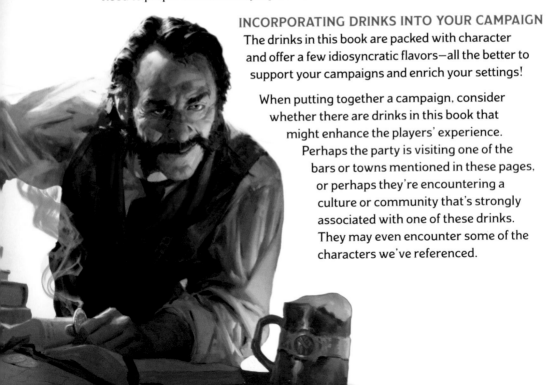

## INCORPORATING DRINKS INTO YOUR CAMPAIGN

The drinks in this book are packed with character and offer a few idiosyncratic flavors—all the better to support your campaigns and enrich your settings!

When putting together a campaign, consider whether there are drinks in this book that might enhance the players' experience. Perhaps the party is visiting one of the bars or towns mentioned in these pages, or perhaps they're encountering a culture or community that's strongly associated with one of these drinks. They may even encounter some of the characters we've referenced.

If the adventurers are encountering sea elves, a round of briny Seafoam cocktails (page 93) garnished with nori may be enriching. If the characters are investigating a mystery at the Pink Flumph, offer them a Fol-de-rol (page 64), and if they're venturing into Evereska, offer them a Moonrise (page 88)! If the characters are fighting a necromancer, serve them a Necromancer (page 22)! Keep in mind that while many of these drinks have their roots in specific communities or character classes, none of the drinks are exclusively enjoyed by just those communities!

The stories shared in this book may even inspire your adventures, and the drinks tied to those stories may come into play. Perhaps drinks that don't have magic properties in our world actually do have magic properties in the characters' world!

## A NOTE ON RESPONSIBLE DRINKING

Drinking is meant to be a pleasurable experience for you and for everyone around you. Please know your limits, exercise moderation, and listen to your friends when they suggest you slow down! Remember that mutual respect is a vital part of every adventuring party, and no one should ever feel pressured to drink if they choose not to.

This book includes nonalcoholic drinks for those who do not drink or for those who choose not to drink, whether forever, for a month, for a night, or for a round.

Don't drink and delve. (But do drink and roleplay as a dungeon delver.)

# SETTING UP A HOME BAR

Any adventurer knows they need to get all the right equipment before setting off on a quest. Being a great host is no different, but you can set aside the bedroll, tinderbox, and 50 feet of hempen rope for this adventure. Here are the tools and tips you'll need to set up a great home bar!

## BAR EQUIPMENT

Many of the tools you will need for these recipes are things you probably already have in your kitchen, such as a **cutting board**, a **small sharp knife**, a **saucepan**, a **citrus peeler**, a **fork or squeezer** to juice a lemon or a lime, a **corkscrew**, a **bottle opener**, and an **ice cube tray**. There are also a few more cocktail-specific tools listed below. If you're missing any of these staples, head out on a quest to get them.

**STRAINER:** Strainers are used for a variety of tasks in these recipes. When you're making syrups or infused alcohols, you'll often use fine-mesh strainers to remove the solids. You'll also need a cocktail strainer to prevent ice from tumbling into your glass when pouring a mixed drink, but if you don't have that, you can use a tea strainer, the lid of your shaker, or just a gentle, steady pouring hand.

**JIGGER:** A jigger allows you to measure out ingredients. A standard jigger holds 1.5 ounces of liquid and may have markings on the inside or outside to show smaller amounts. A double-sided jigger may hold 2 ounces on one side and 1 ounce on the other. Always check the precise measurements on your jigger so you know that you're portioning your drinks correctly.

**FUNNEL:** A funnel is helpful for decanting ingredients into bottles and for pouring mixtures through cheesecloth.

**BAR SPOON:** A bar spoon is a long-handled spoon used for mixing drinks. Its length ensures that you can reach the bottom of the mixing glass to stir all the ingredients. You can stir your drink with a regular tablespoon if you don't have a bar spoon.

**MIXING GLASS:** This is essentially a cocktail-specific pitcher. It's great to have in a home bar, but if you're without one, you can use a regular pitcher or the base of a cocktail shaker in its place.

**CHEESECLOTH (OR FILTER PAPER):** Used to strain solids from fat-washed spirits. See Cat's Cradle (page 43) and Eldritch Storm (page 80).

**MUDDLER:** This is a wooden tool used to crush herbs or fruit in a glass. You can use the handle of a wooden spoon in a pinch.

**COCKTAIL SHAKER:** This is a must for your mixology adventure ahead! A shaker is your basic tool for mixing cocktails.

**SWING-TOP GLASS BOTTLES:** If you think you might want to store leftover cocktails or home-made ingredients like syrups, swing-top glass bottles are very handy. They're airtight, they're reusable, and you can stick them in the dishwasher. A swing-top bottle is also essential for the Harpell's Reserve (page 45), along with an oak infusion spiral, unless you have your own oak barrel!

## GLASSWARE

There are five types of cocktail glassware and two other types of vessels required for the drinks in this book.

**COCKTAIL GLASS:** Cocktails served straight up—chilled with ice and strained into an empty glass—are served in wide stemware glasses with a 6- to 8-ounce capacity. A martini glass is a cocktail glass with straight, flared sides. A coupe is a cocktail glass with rounded sides. You can use these interchangeably. The stem is vital as it stops the drink from losing its chill in your hand.

**FLUTES:** Drinks that include sparkling wine are generally served in a flute, which is a tall, narrow, stemmed glass that retains bubbles for longer.

**HIGHBALL OR COLLINS GLASS:** Cocktails served long—stirred in the glass with lots of ice and mixer—are served in a tall 12-ounce glass called a highball or Collins glass. A highball is wider than a Collins glass. You don't need to own both and can generally use them interchangeably—the larger glass simply holds more ice or can hold more generous garnishes!

**PINT GLASS:** Drinks that include beer, mead, or cider are generally served in a pint or beer glass.

**ROCKS OR OLD-FASHIONED GLASS:** Spirit-forward cocktails are served in rocks or old-fashioned glasses, which are 8- to 10-ounce stemless glasses about as tall as a teacup.

**HEATPROOF CUPS:** For hot drinks such as Candlekeep Tea (page 26), Littlewinter (page 114), Cat's Cradle (page 43), and Illuskan Mulled Cider (page 164), you will need heatproof cups or glasses. Coffee mugs are fine!

**PITCHER:** For the many batch drinks provided in this book, you'll need a pitcher or a punch bowl and a ladle.

## TIPS AND TECHNIQUES

**ALWAYS HAVE ICE READY.** Mixing cocktails requires a good supply of ice, so make sure to fill your ice cube trays in advance of having guests over. Bagged ice is typically low quality and not ideal for cocktails, but it will do in a pinch.

**KEEP THINGS FRESH LONGER BY UTILIZING YOUR FRIDGE.** Vermouth should be kept in the fridge once opened, as should any homemade syrups. Citrus fruit can also be stored in the fridge for maximum freshness.

**CHILL YOUR GLASS.** Cold cocktails are best enjoyed from a chilled glass. Keeping some glasses in the freezer means you will always have a chilled glass ready; but when that's not possible, putting your glassware in the freezer about half an hour in advance will work just fine. If you can't chill your glassware that way or if you forget, you can chill a glass by filling it with crushed ice for half a minute.

**RIM YOUR GLASS.** To achieve a rimmed glass, you will need two saucers. Put a little water (or fruit juice, if used in the cocktail) in one saucer and your powder—for instance, chili-lime salt or popping candy—in the other. Rotate the rim of the glass through the water or juice and then through the powder. Ideally, give the rim a minute to set before pouring in the cocktail.

## BAR STOCK

The main spirits you need for your home bar are gin, bourbon, vodka, dark rum, white rum, brandy, and blanco tequila. Some recipes call for spiced rum, mezcal, or blended scotch. You don't need to buy everything at once; prioritize the spirits or recipes that most appeal to you!

Multiple recipes in this book call for sweet red vermouth, dry white vermouth, orange liqueur, elderflower liqueur, amaretto, or dark amaro, all of which are staples of cocktail making. Aromatic bitters are also essential, with some recipes specifically calling for chocolate or orange bitters.

Many alcoholic ingredients appear in just one or two recipes in this book. These include maraschino liqueur, violet liqueur, coffee liqueur, absinthe, and falernum. Invest in these ingredients as needed rather than keeping them in stock, and make substitutions to a recipe where necessary! (See Adapting Recipes, page 13.)

## PANTRY ITEMS

Most of the nonalcoholic ingredients in these cocktails are easy to find and may already be in your kitchen, but you may need to go a little further for specialty ingredients like butterfly pea powder, nori, edible glitter, pink peppercorns, or popping boba.

Purchase fresh garnishes like limes, lemons, herbs, and olives only when you know you're going to use them, as they don't keep well for too long.

Where a recipe calls for fresh fruit, frozen fruit is often an acceptable substitute. When a recipe calls for juice, you can buy it or press your own.

## ADAPTING RECIPES

All the recipes in this book have been designed and tested for a specific flavor profile, but that does not mean you can't make changes. As in Dungeons & Dragons, once you have a clear idea of how things work, you can introduce adaptations to suit your own preferences and desires and use this book to inspire you rather than to restrict you.

Most of the recipes in this book serve two. Split them in half to serve one! Double them to serve four! It's easier than calculating attack rolls!

If a recipe calls for a spirit or liquor that you don't have, try switching it with an ingredient of similar alcoholic strength. It is generally easier to switch clear spirits for other clear spirits and brown spirits for other brown spirits, but sometimes switching whiskey for gin or rum for tequila just works.

You can try swapping sweet, fortified wines like sweet vermouth, sherry, and port for each other. You can swap dry vermouth for dry sherry or a dry white wine. One fruit liqueur can be swapped for another, one creamy liqueur can be swapped for another, and one herbal liqueur or bitter amaro can be swapped for another, but don't mix between these categories.

If you have made a cocktail and do not like the taste, there are some simple fixes you can try. If the drink is too bitter or acidic, add sugar syrup. If it is too sweet, add lemon or lime juice. If it is too strong, add soda water or more ice, or milk if it's a cream cocktail.

# GIN <small>FROM</small> THE HEARTH <small>IN</small> CANDLEKEEP

The great library fortress of Candlekeep boasts a collection of lore and wisdom that calls to scholars far and wide. Many of its students spend years in the library's stacks, barely venturing beyond the fortress walls.

Thankfully, Candlekeep has its own fest hall to entertain its residents, a traditional tavern called the Hearth, with ink-stained blackwood boards, faded tapestries from long-dead kingdoms, and discrete nooks where patrons can hide away with an ancient spell tome or a trashy penny dreadful. Gin is a popular drink at the Hearth, with different botanical blends passed down like arcane lore and tattered handwritten recipes still sometimes found tucked into old books. Gin was first created as a healing juniper-infused tonic, with various alchemical scholars adding citrus, cardamom, angelica, and other botanicals like rose, coriander, lavender, or cinnamon to enhance the recipe. At some point the quest for medicine became secondary to the quest for a good martini.

# INKPOT NEGRONI

To enter Candlekeep, a would-be scholar must present a written work that the library does not already possess—a significant challenge given that Candlekeep has perhaps the most extensive collection of books and lore in all of Faerûn. Whenever a new arrival comes to the gates with an offering, runners are dispatched to search the stacks and make sure the offered text is unique.

Experts in the culinary arts may have some advantage here, as a book of original recipes counts as a written work. At least one seeker has been granted entry to Candlekeep by sitting for 3 days on a rock in front of the keep and writing down recipes. All the recipes were his own innovations, and one was for this radical cocktail with dark vinegar and a tarragon garnish that was intended to resemble a Candlekeep inkpot with a quill.

## SERVES 2

| | | |
|---|---|---|
| 12 BLACKBERRIES | 2 OUNCES DARK AMARO, SUCH AS CYNAR, FERNET, BRAULIO, AVERNA, DELL'ETNA (SEE COOK'S NOTE) | LARGE ICE CUBES, FOR SERVING |
| 2 OUNCES GIN | | 2 FRESH TARRAGON SPRIGS, FOR GARNISH |
| 2 OUNCES CAMPARI | ROUGHLY CRACKED OR SMALL ICE CUBES | 6 BLACKBERRIES, FOR GARNISH |

In a mixing glass, muddle the blackberries to break them down completely. Add the gin, Campari, and amaro. Fill the mixing glass halfway with ice. Using a long-handled spoon, stir the contents quickly until the spirits are well chilled, about 30 seconds. Place 1 to 2 large ice cubes into two small jars or rocks glasses. Strain and divide the mixture evenly between the two glasses. Garnish each with a tarragon sprig and 3 blackberries. Serve at once.

COOK'S NOTE Amaro is an Italian digestif infused with any number of herbs, roots, flowers, bark, spices, and/or citrus peels. While every amaro producer has their own proprietary recipe that can include dozens of ingredients, these liqueurs are usually bittersweet (though some more bracingly bitter than others!) with a syrupy consistency. Here, we recommend a dark amaro for both color and depth of flavor. Try Averna for a more cola-like sweetness or Fernet if you have a taste for black licorice and the ultra-astringent.

Firstly

Endeavor to procure the finest ingredients

12 Blackberries

2 ounces gin

2 ounces campari

2 ounces dark amaro
such as Cynar, Fernet, Braulio, Averna, del Etna

Roughly cracked or small ice cubes

Large ice cubes, for serving

Tarragon sprigs, for garnish

Secondly

# ASTRAL PLANE

A group of young scribes studying under the archmage Sylvira Savikas were sent on a search in the outer planes to recover a disintegrating tome stored in a room that had become disconnected from the keep. While out on their mission, the scribes saw colors in the outer plane that they had never seen before. Overcome by a manic need to capture the experience, the young scribes rushed back to the Hearth to compare notes. Soon they were taking turns devising drinks from the bottles behind the bar that might capture the colors that haunted their minds. They were never truly able to re-create that dance of light and magic, but they agreed that the flavor of this cocktail came closest to the way the colors of the astral plane felt.

## SERVES 2

4 OUNCES GIN

1 OUNCE VIOLET LIQUEUR, SUCH AS CRÈME DE VIOLETTE

1 OUNCE ELDERFLOWER LIQUEUR, SUCH AS ST GERMAIN

1½ OUNCES FRESH LEMON JUICE

¼ TEASPOON EDIBLE GLITTER (OPTIONAL; SEE COOK'S NOTE)

ROUGHLY CRACKED OR SMALL ICE CUBES

In a cocktail shaker, combine the gin, violet liqueur, elderflower liqueur, lemon juice, and edible glitter. Fill the shaker halfway with ice. Cover and shake for 30 seconds to chill. Strain and divide the mixture evenly into two chilled coupe or martini glasses. Serve at once.

COOK'S NOTE  While the violet liqueur contributes a mystical purple hue to this cocktail, the addition of edible glitter goes a long way to enhance the ethereal look. Edible glitter can easily be found online or in the cake decorating aisle of a well-stocked grocery or arts and crafts store.

# NECROMANCER

On a survey of the fauna of Toril, the powerful sage Kazryn Nyantani encountered a mad necromancer who kept a beautiful garden of wormwood, juniper, and bitter citrus. She discovered, to her great alarm, that the garden was sustained by the same corpses the necromancer called on to do his terrible bidding!

The necromancer crafted an intoxicating potion infused with the fruits of his garden that he claimed would grant him eternal life. He was wrong, but the drink was delicious, with elegantly balanced notes of citrus and anise and a pale pallor reminiscent of the ghastly flesh of the animated dead. Nyantani brought the recipe back to Candlekeep, where it has put more people on their backs than it has ever raised from the dead.

## SERVES 2

| | | |
|---|---|---|
| ½ OUNCE ABSINTHE | 1½ OUNCES FORTIFIED RED WINE, SUCH AS LILLET ROUGE OR COCCHI ROSA | 1 OUNCE FRESH BLOOD ORANGE JUICE, PLUS 2 THIN SLICES |
| 1½ OUNCES GIN | | |
| 1½ OUNCES ORANGE LIQUEUR, SUCH AS COINTREAU | 1 OUNCE FRESH LEMON JUICE | ROUGHLY CRACKED OR SMALL ICE CUBES |

Into each of two chilled coupe or cocktail glasses, pour ¼ ounce of absinthe. Swirl to rinse the glasses, making sure to tilt them to reach the lip of the glass. Discard the excess and set the glasses aside (see Cook's Note).

Fill a cocktail shaker with the gin, orange liqueur, fortified red wine, lemon juice, and blood orange juice. Fill it halfway with ice, cover, and shake to chill, about 30 seconds. Strain and divide the mixture between two glasses. Garnish each glass with a blood orange wheel and serve at once.

**COOK'S NOTE** Rinsing a glass with a spirit is a technique used to impart flavor and aroma without overwhelming the other ingredients in a cocktail. In this instance, absinthe is used to leave a lingering anise scent that is complementary to the bright, citrusy cocktail but not overpowering.

# LIBRARY MARTINI

Varnyr, the senior scribe at Candlekeep, has watched over the books at the library for centuries with the doting attention of a loving mother. Her one overwhelming desire in life is to protect her books. In her earliest days at the library, she planted sage bushes all around Candlekeep. Oil and smoke from the leaves of the sage plant were a natural preventative against the moths and weevils that might have devoured the pages of her books.

Over time, the monks of Candlekeep devised magic means to protect the books instead. The sage plants are now part of the scenery and an integral feature of Candlekeep in many students' minds. Wearing a sage posy or sage embroidery is one way that students might identify each other. The sage-infused Library Martini is one of the most enjoyable ways that Candlekeep uses its excess of sage and honors its history, and it remains a favorite drink of Varnyr's to this day.

## SERVES 2

| SAGE-INFUSED GIN (SEE COOK'S NOTE) 12 OUNCES GIN | 3 SPRIGS FRESH SAGE, LEAVES PLUCKED AND CHOPPED COARSELY, PLUS 2 LEAVES FOR GARNISH 1 STRIP LEMON PEEL | 2 OUNCES DRY VERMOUTH SMALL ICE CUBES |

*To make the sage-infused gin:* In a medium jar, combine the gin, chopped sage, and lemon peel. Cover, shake well, and store in a cool, dry place for at least 24 hours and up to 4 days, shaking and tasting daily to check on strength of the infusion. Once the gin has reached the desired flavor, strain the solids and return it to the jar. Store any remaining infused gin indefinitely.

In a mixing glass, combine 4 ounces of the sage-infused gin and the vermouth. Add the ice and stir with a long-handled spoon until well chilled, about 30 seconds. Strain and divide the mixture evenly into martini or cocktail glasses. Top each with a sage leaf for garnish and serve at once.

COOK'S NOTE Infusing a spirit is not nearly as complicated as it may seem! Simply combine the ingredients of which you want to impart flavor with your spirit and let them mingle for a few hours for hot peppers; 1 to 4 days for herbs and stronger-flavored fruits, vegetables, and spices; and 1 to 3 weeks for milder fruits and vegetables. Make sure to shake daily to keep things moving!

# EMERALD DOOR

The Emerald Door is an iconic sight in Candlekeep, the sole entrance to the Inner Ward and the rich depths of the library. Only the truly worthy can enter here, and most seekers at Candlekeep never make it through that door. Its throbbing green glow becomes a taunt and a promise to those students staring across the Court of Air from the windows of the Hearth.

Ordering the cocktail named for the Emerald Door is something of a statement of purpose. This effervescent glass flute of bright flavor and pale green light is a taste of the elevated life beyond the door, of the promise of great wisdom and learning that all seekers aspire to. They may never discover what the world is like beyond the emerald door, but they can experience just a taste.

## SERVES 2

**MATCHA SYRUP**

¼ CUP SUGAR

1 TABLESPOON MATCHA POWDER (SEE COOK'S NOTE)

¼ CUP WATER

1½ OUNCES FRESH LEMON JUICE

2 FRESH MINT SPRIGS, LEAVES PLUCKED, PLUS MORE SPRIGS FOR GARNISH

1 OUNCE GIN

1 OUNCE ELDERFLOWER LIQUEUR, SUCH AS ST GERMAIN

ROUGHLY CRACKED OR SMALL ICE CUBES

CRUSHED ICE, FOR SERVING

CHILLED DRY SPARKLING WINE, SUCH AS CAVA, PROSECCO, OR CHAMPAGNE, FOR TOPPING OFF

*To make the matcha syrup:* In a small saucepan, stir together the sugar and matcha powder until well combined, breaking up any clumps. Whisk in the water and bring to a boil over medium-high heat. Remove from the heat and carefully stir until the sugar has dissolved. Let cool completely before using. Store any remaining matcha syrup in an airtight jar in the refrigerator for up to 1 week.

Fill a cocktail shaker with the lemon juice and mint leaves. Use a muddler to gently bruise and release the mint's fragrance. Add the gin, elderflower liqueur, and ½ ounce of matcha syrup. Fill halfway with ice, cover, and shake to chill, about 30 seconds. Fill two champagne flutes with crushed ice. Strain and divide the mixture evenly between the two glasses and top with sparkling wine. Garnish each glass with a mint sprig and serve at once.

**COOK'S NOTE** Matcha powder can be found in the coffee and tea aisle of your grocery store or online. Ceremonial-grade, first-harvest matcha has the best quality and will impart the brightest green color, though culinary-grade, second-harvest matcha powder will also work in this recipe.

# CANDLEKEEP TEA

Candlekeep Tea is not actually served at the Hearth but rather a few doors down at the smithy of Khe'ril Hammerbind. The story goes that on one particularly ferocious winter storm night, some students, on the brink of death in their drafty bunk rooms, struggled down to the smithy to beg to sleep by the blazing fires of the forge. The grumpy dwarven smithy took pity on the students, allowed them a place on the stones, and made them hot black tea to warm them from the inside.

Word spread of Hammerbind's kindness, and other students joined them that night, bringing with them gifts of strong liquor, exotic herbs, and even sugar and fruit. Hammerbind mixed the offerings to stretch the tea a little further, and Candlekeep Tea was born. Every time a storm hits, the poorest adjutants are welcomed to the forge for warmth, and together with Hammerbind, they make a new tea, a little different every time. The recipe below is a typical example, but everyone is encouraged to add what they can to the pot.

## SERVES 6

| | | |
|---|---|---|
| 1½ CUPS GIN | ½ OUNCE BITTERS | 2 CLOVES |
| ½ CUP ORANGE LIQUEUR, SUCH AS COINTREAU | 12 OUNCES WATER | 1 CINNAMON STICK |
| ½ CUP RED VERMOUTH | 2 EARL GREY TEA BAGS | ¼ CUP SUGAR |
| ¾ CUP FRESH LEMON JUICE | 3 ORANGE SLICES | LEMON SLICES, FOR GARNISH |

In a large, heatproof pitcher, combine the gin, orange liqueur, red vermouth, lemon juice, and bitters.

In a small saucepan, bring the water to a boil over medium-high heat. Add the tea bags, orange slices, cloves, cinnamon stick, and sugar and turn off the heat. Steep for 4 to 6 minutes. Set a fine-mesh strainer over your pitcher and strain the mixture into it. Stir well and pour carefully into tea cups. Garnish with lemon slices and serve at once.

COOK'S NOTE The longer you allow your tea to steep, the stronger and more astringent your cocktail will be.

# MAGIC JAR

Students of darker magic are closely watched by the senior scribes at Candlekeep in case they are tempted into wickedness. The stoic moon elf Vooshadi Moonriver is especially watchful of those adjutants studying Magic Jar, a necromancy spell that allows the caster to transfer their soul into a jar and then possess a nearby target, swapping the target's soul with their own into the same jar.

Magic Jar is a spell with many dangers, most especially the risk of death if the spell is disrupted and a high chance of spiritual corruption from taking control of another person's body. There is even a possibility of the caster or the target's soul becoming forever trapped in the jar.

Vooshadi did not react well when she learned a group of young scholars had devised a gin punch they dubbed "Magic Jar" because, in the words of a student, "It gets you out of your head." Their frivolous disdain for such a serious spell was alarming to the elder scribe. The students begged Vooshadi to at least try their creation, in the spirit of inquiry, and she reluctantly agreed. Vooshadi still won't refer to this drink by its official name, but she does enjoy a Magic Jar when she wants to let her hair down.

## SERVES 6

1½ CUPS GIN

½ CUP FALERNUM
(SEE COOK'S NOTE)

½ CUP PINEAPPLE JUICE

1½ CUPS CARROT JUICE

½ CUP FRESH LEMON JUICE

LARGE ICE CUBES OR
BLOCK ICE

1 CUP GINGER BEER

CRUSHED ICE

CUCUMBER SPEARS,
MINT, STRAWBERRIES, KIWI,
STARFRUIT, EDIBLE FLOWERS,
CHILI-LIME SALT, FOR GARNISH

In a punch bowl or large pitcher, combine the gin, falernum, pineapple juice, carrot juice, and lemon juice. Add the large ice cubes to fill the bowl halfway and top with ginger beer. Stir gently to combine. Fill six small jars halfway with crushed ice and ladle punch into each glass. Top each with sliced cucumbers, mint sprigs, strawberries, kiwi slices, starfruit, edible flowers, and/or chili-lime salt rim.

COOK'S NOTE Falernum is a syrupy liqueur from the island nation of Barbados. Rum-based and infused with lime, sugar, clove, almond, and ginger, falernum is often used in tiki drinks to impart a spiced sweetness to the tropical tipples.

PUNCHEONS & FLAGONS

# REWARDS

Ulraunt, a former Keeper of the Tomes, was famously stingy with praise for his adjutants to the point it impacted their learning. They never knew if they were doing a good job, because "the Old Buzzard" (as he was known) never offered a word of encouragement. Called out for his reticence by his fellow sages, Ulraunt said that it was simply not in his nature to gush but promised to take steps to ensure his adjutants knew they were doing a good job. He still withheld from giving praises, but he started to send little boxes of strawberry rhubarb tartlets to his best performing students.

Ulraunt is long gone from Candlekeep, but his "rewards" live on at the Hearth and are still sometimes ordered by proud sages. The difference now, of course, is that students can also reward themselves, even when they're doing a terrible job, and now you can too.

=== MAKES 6 ===

ALL-PURPOSE FLOUR, FOR DUSTING

1 SHEET FROZEN PUFF PASTRY, THAWED

4 OUNCES RHUBARB, TRIMMED AND SLICED ¼ INCH THICK

4 OUNCES FRESH STRAWBERRIES, HULLED, HALVED, AND SLICED ¼ INCH THICK

¼ CUP SUGAR

1 TEASPOON PURE VANILLA EXTRACT

2 TEASPOONS CORNSTARCH

½ TABLESPOON FRESH LEMON JUICE

⅛ TEASPOON KOSHER SALT

1 LARGE EGG, LIGHTLY BEATEN

On a gently floured surface, lay down the sheet of puff pastry. Roll the pastry out to ⅛-inch thickness and use a quart container or a bowl with a roughly 5½-inch diameter to cut out 6 circles. Transfer the circles into the cups of a muffin tin, gently pushing down the bottom and crimping the sides to fit.

In a medium bowl, gently stir the rhubarb, strawberries, sugar, vanilla extract, cornstarch, lemon juice, and salt to combine. Using a ¼-cup measure, scoop the filling into the muffin cups. Brush the exposed edges of puff pastry with egg wash and place the tarts into the freezer to chill for 30 minutes.

Preheat the oven to 400°F.

Bake the tarts for 25 minutes, until the edges are golden and the filling is bubbling. Place on a wire rack and let cool before serving.

# WHISKEY FROM
# THE GILDED HORSESHOE INN
# IN LONGSADDLE

The Gilded Horseshoe sits in a very small village far from any major settlements, but it serves a vast area, as this is the establishment of choice for the ranchers on the plains surrounding Longsaddle. That clientele guarantees a lot of rowdy nights on the sawdust-scattered floorboards of this converted barn, but the nearby presence of the powerful Harpell family ensures nothing too destructive ever happens— unless the Harpells are the ones causing trouble. Travelers on the Long Road will find a warm welcome, a sense of safety, and a boot-scootin' night to remember at the Horseshoe, so long as they stay on the right side of the Harpells!

Whiskey made from local Dessarin Valley grain is the drink of choice for locals at the Horseshoe. Usually that means a shot with a beer, but the inn also serves fine whiskey cocktails for fancy merchants, guests of the Harpells, and ranchers with refined tastes!

# HAND OF VECNA

Vecna is a powerful archlich known to some as the Undying King, the Whispered One, and the Master of the Spider Throne. Vecna studied the dark arts from childhood at the knee (or under the boot heel) of his cruel hedge witch mother. Unshackled from the bounds of time and space, Vecna's terrible touch may be as inevitable as death itself.

The archlich's withered hand, also unstuck from time, is a legendarily powerful artifact that grants its bearer terrible necromantic abilities at the cost of the bearer's own hand and eventually at the cost of their life.

While awaiting the inevitable end of all things in Vecna's wrinkled gray clutches, one might as well enjoy this deliciously smoky and potentially sacrilegious cocktail, created either in tribute to a dastardly figure or as a rebuke to a sinister bogeyman.

## SERVES 2

½ OUNCE ABSINTHE
OR PERNOD

2 CUBES OR 2 TEASPOONS
CANE SUGAR

6 DASHES ANGOSTURA
BITTERS

4 OUNCES BLENDED SCOTCH,
PREFERABLY PEATED

ROUGHLY CRACKED OR
SMALL ICE CUBES

LARGE ICE CUBES, TO SERVE

ORANGE PEEL AND STAR
ANISE, FOR GARNISH

Pour ¼ ounce of absinthe into each of two rocks glasses. Swirl to rinse, making sure to tilt them to reach the lip of the glass. Discard the excess and set the glasses aside (see Cook's Note on page 22).

In a mixing glass, muddle the sugar into the angostura bitters to break down the sugar until they have reached a syrupy consistency, adding a few drops of water if needed. Add the scotch to the mixing glass and fill it halfway with ice. Using a long-handled spoon, stir until well chilled, about 30 seconds. Add the large cubes to the rocks glasses. Strain and divide the mixture evenly between the two glasses. Garnish with orange peel and star anise. Serve at once.

COOK'S NOTE  Peated scotch obtains its signature intensity and smokiness from the process of drying barley, when peat—a mixture of decayed vegetation—is burnt to halt the malting process. The smoke penetrates the grain, remaining present in the final product.

# NETHER GOLD

For three thousand years, the Netheril Empire dominated Faerûn from wonderous citadels floating high above the land. Such was the power of the Empire that it seemed indestructible, and that—of course—was its undoing. Karsus, the greatest of the city's spellcasters, was so drunk on power that he tried to place himself among the gods themselves. He was cast down for his pride as was the Empire.

The vast deserts of Anauroch beyond Evereska are the graveyard of Netheril. Treasure hunters often venture out to seek their fortune, hoping to find gold, jewels, or long-lost magic artifacts. Beyond the environmental challenges of the desert and the rivalry of other hunters in a lawless land, they face a high likelihood of death thanks to Netherese creatures, traps, and ancient spells scattered across the sands. The Gilded Horseshoe is the last stop before the desert for many of these hunters. This golden cocktail with honey is often their last drink before they depart, and perhaps their last drink ever.

## SERVES 2

| HONEY SYRUP | 4 SLICES FRESH, PEELED GINGER | ROUGHLY CRACKED OR SMALL ICE CUBES |
| --- | --- | --- |
| ¼ CUP WATER | 4 OUNCES BLENDED SCOTCH | LARGE ICE CUBES |
| ⅓ CUP HONEY | 1½ OUNCES FRESH LEMON JUICE | ½ OUNCE PEATED SCOTCH OR ABSINTHE |
| 1 CHAMOMILE TEA BAG | 2 DASHES BITTERS | |

*To make the honey syrup:* In a small saucepan, bring the water and honey to a boil over high heat. Add the tea bag and turn off the heat. Steep for 10 minutes. Remove the tea bag and allow it to fully cool before using. Store any remaining honey syrup in an airtight jar in the refrigerator for up to 1 week.

In a cocktail shaker, muddle the ginger to partially break it down to release the flavor. Add the blended scotch, lemon juice, 1½ ounces of chamomile honey syrup, and the bitters to the cocktail shaker. Fill halfway with ice, cover, and shake until well chilled, about 30 seconds. Add the large cubes to the rocks glasses. Strain and divide the mixture evenly between the two glasses. Pour ¼ ounce of the peated scotch over the back of a spoon into each glass, allowing the spirit to float on top of the mixed cocktail. Serve at once.

**COOK'S NOTE** Floating is a technique that is used to create layers of flavor within a drink. By gently pouring the ingredient over the back of a spoon, the weight of the spirit is more evenly distributed. This way, it doesn't immediately sink or mix into the other components. Choosing a higher-alcohol, lower-sugar spirit is important here.

# OGRETOE

The ogre Orgo Beardlichen stumbled into the Horseshoe one evening, claiming to have been caught in a freak snowstorm on an otherwise bright, sunny day. The staff warmed him up but could not save the big toe on his left foot, which had already turned black. Orgo took an axe off the wall, chopped off the toe, and plopped it in a cask of whiskey. He said he would find a healer who could reattach it. There had been no freak snowstorm, however. Orgo had merely offended a frost druid, and she wasn't done taking her revenge on him. The druid entered the bar and killed Orgo on the spot. The toe in the whiskey was the only part of him left behind.

Drinking the ogre toe whiskey became a strange tradition at the Horseshoe. People dared each other to drink a shot of contaminated whiskey with the toe bobbing in the glass, and anyone who "kissed" the toe was inducted into "the Ogretoe Society." Unfortunately, the adventurer Volothamp Geddarm swallowed the toe, and now the bar serves a drink that approximates the original with a pickle in place of the toe and pickle juice to give it that ogre-ish flavor.

## SERVES 2

4 OUNCES WHISKEY

1 OUNCE DRY VERMOUTH

1 OUNCE PICKLE JUICE

1 OUNCE FRESH LEMON JUICE

ROUGHLY CRACKED OR SMALL ICE CUBES

FRESH DILL, FOR GARNISH

PICKLE, SLICED CROSSWISE, OR CORNICHONS, FOR GARNISH

In a cocktail shaker, combine the whiskey, vermouth, pickle juice, and lemon juice. Fill the shaker halfway with ice. Cover and shake until well chilled, about 30 seconds. Fill two rocks glasses halfway with ice. Strain and divide the mixture evenly between glasses. Garnish with dill and pickles. Serve at once.

# PEGASUS

Many remarkable creatures are found in the Ivy Mansion, the ancestral home of the Harpells, a powerful wizard family. Rumor has it that those animals don't roam freely: they've been shrunken down and placed in glass jars as part of the family's collection of magic experiments and wonders. There may be a Pegasus or two in the collection, but the Harpells don't like to see these magic winged horses fall into rival hands. When a group of vicious hunters came to the Moonwood to hunt for Pegasuses, the Harpells called on the legendary orcish druid Dawan Pax, also known as "the Hunter's Curse," to stop them.

Pax made short work of the Moonwood hunters and brought the injured Pegasuses to Ivy Mansion to establish a sanctuary. Pax also left behind a flask of invigorating fruit tonic that became the basis for a cocktail to raise funds for the care of the creatures. The Harpells thanked him and hurried him away before he could learn of the glass jars in their barn.

## SERVES 2

| GINGER SYRUP | 4 SLICES FRESH PEACH (SEE COOK'S NOTE) | 4 OUNCES BOURBON |
|---|---|---|
| ¼ CUP PEELED, SLICED FRESH GINGER | 12 FRESH MINT LEAVES, PLUS 2 SPRIGS FOR GARNISH | ROUGHLY CRACKED OR SMALL ICE CUBES |
| ¼ CUP SUGAR | 1 OUNCE FRESH LEMON JUICE | CRUSHED ICE |
| ¼ CUP WATER | | 2 DASHES BITTERS |

*To make the ginger syrup:* In a small saucepan, bring the ginger, sugar, and water to a boil over medium-high heat. Lower the heat and bring the mixture to a simmer. Cover and simmer for 10 minutes. Turn off the heat and steep for 30 minutes. Let the syrup fully cool before using. Store any remaining ginger syrup in an airtight jar in the refrigerator for up to 1 week.

In a mixing glass, muddle the peaches, mint leaves, and lemon juice until the peaches are well broken down. Add 1 ounce of ginger syrup and the bourbon and fill halfway with ice. Using a long-handled spoon, stir until well chilled, about 30 seconds. Completely fill two highball glasses with crushed ice. Strain and divide the mixture evenly between the two glasses. Top with a dash of bitters and garnish with a mint sprig. Serve at once.

COOK'S NOTE If you want to make this cocktail outside of peach season, frozen peaches work just as well! Simply fully thaw before using to enjoy vibrant peach flavor all year long.

# CAT'S CRADLE

Any bar or tavern that plays host to occasional tabaxi travelers would be advised to have some version of this milk punch on their menu. Tabaxi are a catlike people who share a curiosity about the world that inspires them to travel far and wide. Most wandering tabaxi are also adept hunters, so while they may enjoy a steaming cup of gristly brown tavern stew, they don't necessarily need to part with coin to get fed. They don't even pay for a room, as they'd rather sleep curled in a sunbeam by the window or in front of a roaring fire. This is very frustrating for innkeepers, who don't like to see any traveler pass by without some payment. That's where milk punch comes in. There is something nostalgic about milk. It ensures sweet dreams for a tabaxi far from home. Spiking that milk with a little whiskey, well, perhaps that makes those dreams come a little quicker!

## SERVES 6

| | | |
|---|---|---|
| 4 WHOLE CLOVES | PEEL OF 1 LEMON | ½ CUP PINEAPPLE JUICE |
| 4 GREEN CARDAMOM PODS | ¼ CUP SUGAR | 1½ CUPS WHISKEY |
| 1 CINNAMON STICK | ¼ CUP FRESH LEMON JUICE | ¼ OUNCE BITTERS |
| 1 STAR ANISE | 1 CUP STRONG BREWED CHAI TEA | 1 CUP MILK |
| ¼ TEASPOON CORIANDER SEEDS | | LARGE ICE CUBES |

In a small skillet, toast the cloves, cardamom pods, cinnamon, star anise, and coriander seeds over medium-low heat for 2 to 3 minutes, until fragrant. Remove from the heat.

In a medium bowl, combine the lemon peels, sugar, and toasted spices. Muddle the ingredients together for about 30 seconds to release oils from the lemon peels. Add the lemon juice, tea, pineapple juice, whiskey, and bitters. Allow to sit for at least 1 hour to infuse flavors.

After the hour-long infusion, in a small saucepan over medium heat, bring the milk to a bare simmer. Remove from the heat and pour into a separate medium bowl. Gently pour the whiskey mixture into the hot milk while stirring. The milk will curdle immediately. Allow the punch to cool to room temperature. Transfer it to the refrigerator to chill for at least 1 hour and up to 24 hours.

Set a fine-mesh strainer lined with a coffee filter over a clean container. Very slowly pour the curdled liquid into the strainer. A nest of curds will form at the bottom of the strainer; try not to disturb these. Straining may take several hours. Once the punch has fully drained, add the large cubes to two rocks glasses. Pour about 4 ounces of the punch evenly between the two glasses.

# HARPELL'S RESERVE

A ll members of the Harpell family are welcome at the Gilded Horseshoe, and their drinks are always free—because all landlords of the Gilded Horseshoe know what happened to former owner Edgourd Mellish generations ago when he asked Lord Morgus Harpell to cover his bar tab. Edgourd now stands in the Harpells' statue garden, wreathed in ivy.

To keep the Harpells happy, there's always a special blend of the Harpell's Reserve in a cask behind the bar. The blend is aged in sacred oak from the Neverwinter Wood, and no one else is allowed to drink it. One fool attempted to jump the bar to sample it and exploded into a cloud of bugs. Another was served the Reserve by mistake and reverted to infancy. An entire group of raiders attempted to rob the bar and almost got away with their heist, but one idiot tried to drink from the barrel and the whole group melted on the spot.

We suggest you attempt this recipe at your own risk.

### SERVES 8

| | | |
|---|---|---|
| CANE SUGAR SYRUP | 24-OUNCE SWING-TOP BOTTLE | 4 TEASPOONS BITTERS, SUCH AS ANGOSTURA |
| ¼ CUP CANE SUGAR | OAK INFUSION SPIRAL (SEE COOK'S NOTE) | LARGE ICE CUBE |
| ¼ CUP WATER | | MARASCHINO CHERRY, SUCH AS LUXARDO |
| | 20 OUNCES BOURBON OR RYE WHISKEY | ORANGE PEEL, FOR GARNISH |

*To make the cane sugar syrup:* In a small saucepan, bring the cane sugar and water to a boil over medium-high heat, stirring as needed until the sugar has completely dissolved. Remove from the heat and allow to fully cool before using. Store any remaining cane sugar syrup in an airtight jar in the refrigerator for up to 1 week.

Place the infusion spiral into the swing-top bottle. Add the bourbon, 2¼ ounces of cane sugar syrup, and bitters. Cover and shake well. Place in a cool, dry place for at least 48 hours and up to 1 week, shaking daily and checking for oak flavor. When the cocktail has reached the desired intensity, shake well once more and add a large ice cube to a rocks glass. Pour 2½ ounces of cocktail mixture over the ice in each glass. Garnish with a Luxardo cherry and orange peel. Serve at once.

COOK'S NOTE  For swing-top bottles, an infusion spiral is the quickest way to get some age into a cocktail. You can also achieve the same aging result with a small barrel. Personal oak aging barrels can easily be found online in a variety of sizes. Just increase the batch size to accommodate the size of your barrel and allow it to rest for 3 to 4 weeks.

# LOKLEE

On the occasion of the Grand Duke of Baldur's Gate, Ulder Ravengard's, civic visit to Longsaddle, the Lord of Longsaddle, Dowell Harpell, instructed one of the bartenders at the Gilded Horseshoe to make a cocktail in his honor.

The bartender, a githyanki named L'rai, was born in Baldur's Gate and knew of the city's darkness, sophistication, and complexity very well. She created a cocktail inspired by her memories of a sour-edged and very strong bathtub whiskey rumored to have been made and enjoyed by shepherds since the time when Baldur's Gate was still the humble village known as Loklee. Unfortunately, Lord Ravengard never bothered to visit the tavern during his stay to try L'rai's adaptation. The Gilded Horseshoe still serves the Loklee cocktail in case he ever stops by.

## SERVES 2

4 OUNCES BOURBON

1½ OUNCES SWEET VERMOUTH

1 OUNCE AMARO, SUCH AS CYNAR, FERNET, BRAULIO, AVERNA, OR DELL'ETNA

½ TEASPOON BALSAMIC VINEGAR

2 DASHES ORANGE BITTERS

ROUGHLY CRACKED OR SMALL ICE CUBES

ORANGE PEEL, FOR GARNISH

In a mixing glass, combine the bourbon, sweet vermouth, amaro, balsamic vinegar, and bitters. Fill the glass halfway with ice and stir with a long-handled spoon until well chilled, about 30 seconds. Strain and divide the mixture evenly into two cocktail glasses or coupes. Garnish with an orange peel and serve at once.

# DRAGONBERRIES

The warlock Zanizyre Clockguard has a fearsome reputation because of her bond to her patron Tiamat, the terrible Queen of Dragons. When Zanizyre passed through Longsaddle, even the Harpells were a little nervous, despite the fact that she is really one of the nicest gnomes you'll ever meet.

Zanizyre came to the Gilded Horseshoe with three hungry hatchling dragons that she had rescued from an Auranoch cyclops. The kitchen was closed and the larders were nearly empty, but the staff were determined not to anger Tiamat. They found some barrels of chickpeas, added a few spices, and asked Zanizyre to provide the fire to roast them into a delicious crunchy snack. The baby dragons loved the snack, as did Zanizyre herself. She left a generous tip and told the bar staff that Tiamat might spare them on her inevitable return to this world if they kept the dragonberries on the menu.

## SERVES 4

2 CANS OF CHICKPEAS, DRAINED AND RINSED

1½ TEASPOONS GROUND CUMIN

1½ TEASPOONS GROUND PAPRIKA

½ TEASPOON CHILI POWDER

½ TEASPOON GROUND CORIANDER

½ TEASPOON GARLIC POWDER OR GRANULATED GARLIC

½ TEASPOON ONION POWDER

¼ TEASPOON CAYENNE PEPPER

1 TEASPOON SALT

3 TABLESPOONS EXTRA-VIRGIN OLIVE OIL

Preheat the oven to 425°F. Line a baking sheet with aluminum foil.

Spread the drained chickpeas over a layer of paper towels or a dish towel. Layer another towel on top of the chickpeas and pat them dry. Transfer them into a medium bowl and add the cumin, paprika, chili powder, coriander, garlic powder, onion powder, cayenne pepper, salt, and olive oil. Toss to coat.

Spread the chickpeas in a single layer on the prepared baking sheet. Bake for 25 to 35 minutes, until crispy. Remove from the oven and let fully cool before serving.

# VODKA FROM
## THE PINK FLUMPH THEATER
## IN WATERDEEP

One of the hottest tickets in Waterdeep, the Pink Flumph Theater is a gaudy performance hall that puts on plays and entertainments every afternoon and evening. The theater is often packed with folks eager to witness the magic special effects generated by the Flumph's resident faerie dragon, Wishes. Any bard passing through Waterdeep dreams of booking a gig here—and hopefully getting a share of the night's takings at the bar!

The proprietor of the Pink Flumph, Iokaste Daliano, has an arrangement with a local vodka distillery that says it makes its vodka from a healing spring. Many patrons report feeling wonderful on its effects—until they wake up the next morning.

-VODKA-
DISTILLED LOCALLY FOR

The
PINK FLUMPH
THEATER

USING ONLY THE
PUREST WATERS FROM
THE CLEARWELL

# HORDELANDER

Iokaste was once briefly smitten with a gentleman named Gannis Frostmantle who visited Waterdeep and claimed to be an emissary of the Tuigan horde from the distant lands of the Endless Waste. Gannis courted the widow and asked her help in finding people to fund his campaign against demonic intruders. He insisted he did not need her money, of course, but she would not hear of his refusal. A well-traveled woman, Iokaste added a drink to the menu of the Flumph that would remind Gannis of home: a salted yogurt-based drink that was popular among the horse riders of the Hordelands. Gannis tried the drink and spat it out, and that was when Iokaste realized he was a fraud.

In a rare instance of solidarity between Iokaste and Wishes, they arranged a visit for Gannis with the wrathful gods of the Hordelands—or at least an illusory approximation. Gannis was last seen heading for Luskan. The Hordelander cocktail remained on the menu as Iokaste had developed a taste for saltiness.

### SERVES 2

1 CUP PLAIN GREEK YOGURT

3 OUNCES VODKA

2 OUNCES FRESH LEMON JUICE

8 FRESH MINT LEAVES, PLUS 2 SPRIGS FOR GARNISH

¼ TEASPOON BLACK PEPPER

1 TEASPOON KOSHER SALT

½ CUP SODA WATER

ROUGHLY CRACKED OR SMALL ICE CUBES

In a blender, blend together the yogurt, vodka, lemon juice, mint, black pepper, and salt until smooth. Add the soda water to the blender and stir well. Fill two highball glasses halfway with ice and divide the mixture evenly between the two glasses. Garnish each glass with a mint sprig and serve at once.

# CHEAP SEAT

Wishes, the iridescent violet faerie dragon brought to Waterdeep from Kara-Tur, is credited as the secret of the Pink Flumph's success. It's Wishes's illusory magic that enhances the performances on the stage, creating special effects like wild weather, the din of clashing armies, and the floral perfume of a faerie bough. Unfortunately, some nights Wishes just doesn't feel inspired. Ever since his friend Algondar died and Iokaste took over, Wishes has been haunted by grief and frustrated by Iokaste's disinterest in the arts. Some nights Wishes just turns invisible and hides under the stage.

Thankfully, the performers devised a way to entice Wishes out with nut butter. Specifically, the nut butter rim of a Cheap Seat cocktail, a delicious creamy, chocolatey treat that's a little sweet, a little bitter, and very inspiring. One of these usually guarantees a show, and three of them guarantee a performance.

---

## SERVES 2

2 TEASPOONS ALMOND, CASHEW, OR PEANUT BUTTER

3 OUNCES VODKA

2 OUNCES DARK CRÈME DE CACAO OR CHOCOLATE LIQUEUR

1 OUNCE DARK AMARO, SUCH AS CYNAR, FERNET, BRAULIO, AVERNA, OR DELL'ETNA

1 OUNCE IRISH CREAM

4 DASHES CHOCOLATE BITTERS

ROUGHLY CRACKED OR SMALL ICE CUBES

½ TEASPOON COCOA POWDER

---

Spread 1 teaspoon of almond butter around the top inner edge of two cocktail glasses with the back of a spoon. Set aside.

In a cocktail shaker, combine the vodka, dark crème de cacao, amaro, Irish cream, and bitters. Fill the shaker halfway with ice. Cover and shake until well chilled, about 30 seconds. Strain and divide the mixture evenly between the two glasses. Dust each cocktail with cocoa powder and serve at once.

COOK'S NOTE Despite what its name suggests, crème de cacao doesn't contain milk or cream. The use of the term *crème* here refers to the sugar content of the spirit. Confusingly, there are many chocolate liqueurs that are creamy. Try to avoid using those here, and instead opt for a dark chocolate liqueur. If you have only a creamy chocolate spirit on hand, omit the Irish cream and increase the amount of amaro to 2 ounces.

# MALATRAN MULE

Iokaste Daliano requires a strong drink to get her through each night at the Pink Flumph. The truth is, she hates theater. Her late husband, Algondar, created the Flumph to indulge his passion for the arts, and when he died, she kept it open to indulge her own passion, which was hobnobbing with rich and powerful theater patrons and finagling her way into a position of influence in Waterdeep.

In her younger days, Iokaste traveled to Kara-Tur as a treasure hunter. It was there she met the young Algondar, then a traveling bard, and a faerie dragon that could grant Algondar's "wishes" to own a theater. Algondar brought "Wishes" back to Waterdeep to star in his shows, and Iokaste brought back a taste for strong, spicy drinks that could help her endure night after night of raucous flamboyant theatrical entertainments. The Malatran Mule is her contribution to the venue.

## SERVES 2

| LEMONGRASS SYRUP | 2 SLICES OF FRESNO OR THAI CHILE (OPTIONAL) | 10 FRESH CILANTRO LEAVES |
| :---: | :---: | :---: |
| ½ CUP WATER | | 1 OUNCE FRESH LIME JUICE |
| ½ CUP SUGAR | 8 FRESH BASIL LEAVES | ROUGHLY CRACKED OR SMALL ICE CUBES |
| 2 STALKS FRESH LEMONGRASS, SLICED INTO 4-INCH PIECES, HALVED LENGTHWISE, AND LIGHTLY CRUSHED | 8 FRESH MINT LEAVES | 4 OUNCES VODKA |
| | | GINGER BEER |

*To make the lemongrass syrup:* In a small saucepan, bring the water and sugar to a boil over medium-high heat. Add the lemongrass and turn down the heat to low. Cover and simmer for 10 minutes. Turn off the heat and steep for at least 30 minutes, and up to 1 hour. Set a fine-mesh strainer over a heatproof container and pour the syrup through to remove the solids. Let cool completely before using. Store any remaining lemongrass syrup in an airtight jar in the refrigerator for up to 1 week.

In each of the two highball glasses, place 1 chile (if using), 4 basil leaves, 4 mint leaves, and 5 cilantro leaves. Divide the lime juice evenly between the glasses. Using a muddler, bruise the herbs until fragrant. Fill each glass to the top with ice. Add 2 ounces of vodka and ¼ ounce of the lemongrass syrup to each glass. Top with ginger beer and stir gently with a long-handled spoon. Serve at once.

COOK'S NOTE This cocktail is built in the serving glasses rather than combining the ingredients in a mixing glass. This keeps all the intensity and flavor of the herbs in the finished drink, as they are not strained out and can continue to infuse their essence into the finished cocktail.

# NIGHT WATCH

The Harpers are a secret network of magic spies who champion the downtrodden and wage war against tyrants. According to rumor, many of their number are bards, minstrels, actors, musicians, and other performers—which means that in any theater at any given time, there may be a Harper among the cast.

The actor Yaliek Iltizmar, who specializes in playing romantic blackguards and evil princes, has a theory that the surest way to spot a Harper in a theater is to see who's ordering a Night Watch at the aftershow. Harpers are known for their nocturnal vigilance, after all, and this coffee-forward cocktail is a favorite for anyone who wants to stay awake through the night. Yaliek says she always has one eye open to spot which of her fellow performers might be a Harper. Yaliek also often has a Night Watch in hand because, she says, she just likes the taste.

## SERVES 2

| | | |
|---|---|---|
| 2 OUNCES VODKA | 1 OUNCE LICOR 43 OR GRAND MARNIER | ROUGHLY CRACKED OR SMALL ICE CUBES |
| 2 OUNCES COFFEE LIQUEUR | ¾ OUNCE FRESH ORANGE JUICE | ORANGE OR LEMON PEEL, FOR GARNISH |
| 1 OUNCE COLD BREW CONCENTRATE OR ESPRESSO | | |

In a mixing glass, combine the vodka, coffee liqueur, cold brew concentrate, Licor 43, and orange juice. Fill it halfway with ice. Using a long-handled spoon, stir until well chilled, about 30 seconds. Fill two rocks glasses halfway with ice. Strain and divide the mixture evenly between the two glasses. Garnish with an orange peel and serve at once.

COOK'S NOTE Licor 43 is a sweet, Spanish liqueur that has a complex flavor of vanilla, citrus, and various herbs and spices. While there is no direct substitute for Licor 43, bittersweet citrus liqueurs like Grand Marnier achieve a similar result in this cocktail.

# MOTHER

Somewhere between a drink and a meal, "Mother" was created by the Pink Flumph's celebrated performer, the drag queen Chaotic Eva. Eva needed something to keep her nourished and drunk as she gamely made her way through up to fifteen performances a week on the Waterdhavian stage. Eva inspired many drag performers to follow in her footsteps, earning her the honorific Mother, and her name was also transferred to her favorite drink. Most who try it are quickly converted to its charms, though Eva's own drag children—Misty Step, Halflina, and Gary Ooze—are too squeamish to give the drink a try.

## SERVES 2

MIX (MAKES ENOUGH FOR 4 COCKTAILS)

24 OUNCES TOMATO JUICE

6 TABLESPOONS PREPARED HORSERADISH

3 TABLESPOONS WORCESTERSHIRE SAUCE

2 TABLESPOONS HOT SAUCE

4 TABLESPOONS FRESH LEMON OR LIME JUICE

2 TABLESPOONS CAPER, OLIVE, OR PICKLE BRINE

2 TABLESPOONS OYSTER WATER

1 TEASPOON FISH SAUCE (OPTIONAL)

1 TEASPOON KOSHER SALT

1 TEASPOON CELERY SALT

1 TEASPOON COARSELY GROUND BLACK PEPPER

4 OUNCES VODKA

OYSTERS IN WATER, FOR GARNISH

FRESH OR PICKLED VEGETABLES, LEMON OR LIME WEDGES, AND/OR OLIVES, FOR GARNISH

*To make the mix:* In a pitcher or large measuring cup, combine the tomato juice, horseradish, Worcestershire sauce, hot sauce, lemon juice, caper brine, oyster water, fish sauce (if using), kosher salt, celery salt, and black pepper and stir well. Store any remaining mix in an airtight jar in the refrigerator for up to 1 week. Shake well before using.

Fill two highball glasses with ice. Add 4 ounces of the mix and 2 ounces of vodka to each glass and stir with a long-handled spoon. Garnish with an oyster and other garnishes of your choosing. Serve at once.

COOK'S NOTE Though it may seem odd to include these fishy ingredients in a cocktail, the salty, savory nature of these components add just the right amount of umami to the spicy acidity of the tomato base.

# TPK
## (TOTAL PARTY KATASTROPHE)

A s the nights draw down toward winter, the people of Waterdeep mark the changing seasons with an unusually bloody festival called Howldown. The City Guard, accompanied by a few willing Waterdhavians, head out into the surrounding countryside to hunt down and slay any beasts, creatures, monsters, and even criminals who might threaten rural residents of the villages beyond the city walls. The City Watch conducts a similar purge within the walls. It is a cruel, brutal, and very dubious tradition.

Like many establishments, the Pink Flumph hosts a breakfast for returning crews as the sun comes up, complete with pitchers of a delicious fruity punch made with tart tamarind, sweet passion fruit, and bright green slices of kiwi. This "TPK" is the only "total party katastrophe" that a Howldown crew wants to experience after a night of fighting monsters. As the name implies, a TPK can absolutely finish off a whole party.

### SERVES 6

**TAMARIND BASE**

1 MEDIUM FRESH LEMONGRASS STALK, CUT INTO 4-INCH PIECES, HALVED LENGTHWISE AND LIGHTLY CRUSHED

1¼ CUPS WATER

¼ CUP PACKED LIGHT BROWN SUGAR

FRUIT FROM 3 TAMARIND PODS, ABOUT ¼ CUP OR 2½ OUNCES WET TAMARIND BLOCK, TORN INTO PIECES

1 TEASPOON PURE VANILLA EXTRACT

1 CUP PASSION FRUIT JUICE

1 CUP VODKA

½ CUP APEROL

⅓ CUP FRESH LIME JUICE

4 KIWIS, PEELED AND SLICED

1 TABLESPOON POMEGRANATE ARILS

ROUGHLY CRACKED OR SMALL ICE CUBES

*To make the tamarind base:* In a small saucepan over medium heat, bring the lemongrass and water to a boil. Remove from the heat and whisk in the sugar, tamarind, and vanilla, mashing the fruit with the whisk until it is mostly broken down. Allow to sit for 30 minutes. Set a fine-mesh strainer over a heatproof container and pour the liquid through to remove the solids. Let cool fully before using.

In a pitcher or punch bowl, combine 1 cup of the tamarind base, the passion fruit juice, vodka, Aperol, lime juice, sliced kiwis, and pomegranate arils. Using a long-handled spoon, stir to combine. Fill six rocks glasses halfway with ice, add the punch, and serve at once.

COOK'S NOTE  Look for tamarind in processed blocks at your local Mexican or Asian grocery store.

# FOL-DE-ROL

This delightful cherry-red concoction is a favorite among the repertory players at the Flumph. The traveling bard Florizan Blank brought the recipe from his homeland, where it was equally and exclusively beloved by the royal court. That same royal family was tragically slaughtered in a bloody coup a few years prior with the exception of one young prince who was smuggled to safety by his music teacher and reportedly given a new identity. The whereabouts of the prince remain a great mystery.

It is not clear how Florizan came by the recipe for the Fol-de-rol, which was a closely guarded royal secret, but he tells his fellow performers that striding the stage as kings and queens makes them as worthy of the secret as any true monarch. After all, we are all just performing our roles.

### SERVES 2

| | | |
|---|---|---|
| 6 FRESH OR THAWED FROZEN CHERRIES, PITTED | 2 OUNCES MARASCHINO LIQUEUR, SUCH AS LUXARDO | ROUGHLY CRACKED OR SMALL ICE CUBES |
| 4 OUNCES VODKA | 2 OUNCES COCONUT WATER | LUXARDO CHERRIES, FOR GARNISH |
| | 1½ OUNCES FRESH LIME JUICE | |

In a cocktail shaker, use a muddler to break down the cherries until their juices are released. Add the vodka, maraschino liqueur, coconut water, and lime juice. Fill the shaker halfway with ice. Cover and shake until well chilled, about 30 seconds. Place a Luxardo cherry into the bottom of two cocktail glasses. Strain and divide the mixture evenly between the two glasses. Serve at once.

COOK'S NOTE  Make sure to use coconut water and not coconut milk or cream in this cocktail. The fat in coconut milk or cream will solidify when chilled and won't fully incorporate into the other ingredients. Using high-quality, pressed coconut water will pack the most flavorful punch and will keep the drink clear and uniform.

# FLUMPHCAKES

For anyone unsure of what a "Flumph" is, they are strange, floating, jellyfish-like creatures found in the Underdark. Wise, kind, and good-natured, these peculiar creatures feed exclusively on psionic energy. That energy affects their mood, which in turn affects their coloration. A pink flumph is a happy flumph. Darker colors reflect darker emotions and may suggest that the flumphs are feeding off something dangerous, like aboleths or mind flayers, which is a useful warning to explorers.

Flumphcakes are small pancakes that resemble upbeat flumphs in their flatness, roundness, and pale hue. Patrons at the theater can order postshow flumphcakes in a range of colors to match their own mood; pink flumphcakes are served with strawberries, green flumphcakes with cream cheese and chives, and black flumphcakes with caviar. No flumphs are harmed in the making of these cakes.

## SERVES 6

| | | |
|---|---|---|
| 1 CUP ALL-PURPOSE FLOUR | ½ TEASPOON BAKING POWDER | 1 LARGE EGG, SEPARATED |
| ¾ TEASPOON SALT | ¾ CUP BUTTERMILK | 5 TABLESPOONS UNSALTED BUTTER |
| | 1 TABLESPOON SUGAR | |

In large bowl, combine the flour, salt, and baking powder. In a medium bowl, whisk together the buttermilk, sugar, egg yolk, and 1 tablespoon of the butter, melted. Slowly whisk the egg mixture into the flour mixture until the batter is mostly combined; some lumps will remain. Set aside.

In a small bowl, whisk the egg white until aerated and soft peaks form. Gently fold the egg whites into the pancake batter, being careful not to overmix. Let rest for 15 minutes.

Line a wire rack or plate with paper towels. Heat a large skillet over medium heat and melt 1 tablespoon of butter. Scoop 8 dollops, about 1½ tablespoons each, into the skillet, and cook for 1 to 2 minutes, until bubbles rise to the surface. Flip the pancakes over and cook for another 2 minutes, until the edges appear dry and the second side is golden. Transfer to the paper towel–lined wire rack. Add another tablespoon of butter to the skillet and repeat the process until all the batter is used up.

COOK'S NOTE These pancakes can be topped with anything your heart desires! Some ideas include sour cream, chives, finely diced shallots, smoked salmon, trout or other fish roe, grated hard-boiled egg, lemony ricotta, fresh fruit, or jam.

# RUM FROM
# THE LOW LANTERN
# IN BALDUR'S GATE

The boards of this old merchant ship were soaked with rum and blood long before the *Low Lantern* permanently docked in Baldur's Gate. No longer seaworthy, the ship has become one of the most popular taverns and gambling houses in the city, especially beloved by sailors and smugglers who have adjusted to the dim light of a ship's interior and who find some comfort in the tavern's familiar décor of old barrels and knotted ropes.

The gaming tables are always hot here, and rum is the grog of choice, readily supplied and heartily enjoyed by passing traders who trust the discretion of the tavern's proprietor, Laraelra Thundreth, a fellow former seafarer now commonly known as "the Captain."

THE
LOW LANTERN

ACQUIRED
ABROAD

BARREL-AGED
ABOARD

FAIRLY DECENT AGRICOLE
RUM

# SCRIMSHAW

A merchant sailor named Hitoshi Jade often pays his bar tab at the Low Lantern with scrimshaw, an intricate carving on bone or ivory depicting ships at sea, mermaids, sea creatures, long-lost loves, or elegant abstract designs. The artform of scrimshaw has always been popular among sailors on long sea voyages, and Jade is an especially proficient scrimshaw artist, able to etch extraordinary intricate scenes for large amounts of coin. The Captain is an enthusiastic fan of Jade's work and has a cocktail on the menu with bone-white foam, served in an etched coupe glass in tribute to his scrimshaw. Unfortunately for Jade, he's an equally enthusiastic fan of booze, and his bar tab frequently exceeds his coin, so most of his work ends up behind the bar at the Low Lantern to cover his expenses rather than ever going on sale!

## SERVES 2

4 OUNCES LIGHT RUM

1 OUNCE LICOR 43

1 OUNCE FRESH LIME JUICE

1 OUNCE COCONUT CREAM

4 DASHES CHOCOLATE BITTERS

ROUGHLY CRACKED OR
SMALL ICE CUBES

In a cocktail shaker, combine the rum, Licor 43, lime juice, coconut cream, and chocolate bitters. Fill it halfway with ice. Cover and shake until well chilled, about 30 seconds. Double strain the mixture to remove any coconut solids before dividing it evenly between two etched-glass coupes. Serve at once.

COOK'S NOTE  To give this cocktail some additional scrimshaw flair, create a design using cocoa powder and a stencil. Create a stencil by cutting a design from a piece of heavy-weight paper or card stock with a craft knife. Make sure your piece of paper is large enough to rest across the edges of the glass.

# CELEBRATION BREW

This frothy blend of rum, beer, and citrus came to Baldur's Gate with the dwarven diaspora moving from the mountains to the city. A traditional dwarven drink beloved for its golden hue, it feels like a bucket of sunshine in the dingy dark of the underground world, and its popularity has not waned in the new aboveground grayness of the city.

Celebration Brew is not tied to any specific event in dwarven culture. On the contrary, dwarves will order this drink to commemorate anything at all. Discovered a new gold deposit? That's cause for a celebration! Had a new baby? That's cause for a celebration! Lost a shoe? That's cause for a celebration!

The drink is also known as Liquid Courage because there are times when everything is grim and hope is hard to come by. On occasions when there is nothing to celebrate, well, that's when you need some liquid courage to get you through. Any other circumstances? Cause for a celebration!

## SERVES 2

2½ OUNCES DARK SPICED RUM

1½ OUNCES ORANGE LIQUEUR, SUCH AS TRIPLE SEC OR COINTREAU

1 OUNCE FRESH LEMON JUICE

1 OUNCE FRESH ORANGE JUICE

ROUGHLY CRACKED OR SMALL ICE CUBES

1½ CUPS LAGER

2 ORANGE SLICES, TO GARNISH

Add the rum, orange liqueur, lemon juice, and orange juice to a cocktail shaker. Fill the shaker halfway with ice. Cover and shake until well chilled, about 30 seconds. Strain and divide the mixture evenly between two tulip glasses. Top each glass with ¾ cup of lager and gently stir with a long-handled spoon to combine. Garnish with orange slices and serve at once.

# CHULTWATER

The tropical wilderness of Chult is a place so rife with danger that any explorer or traveler returning from the islands is marked with high esteem. Aremag, the dragon turtle, devours ships in the bay; the froglike grungs poison unwary travelers with their darts; wanderers become forever lost in the cursed gardens of Nangalore; and too many fools are crushed, slashed, or devoured by dinosaurs. The treasures and wonders of Chult make it worth the risk, at least for some.

A merchant named Gannis Tath came to the Low Lantern with a wooden box full of rare stones that he hoped to sell to raise funds for an expedition. He met with possible investors at the Lantern and shared an elaborate bowl of rum and juices that he called "Chultwater." He claimed that anyone who shared this traditional drink with him was bound to an unbreakable trust. It was adventurer Artis Cimber who informed the Captain that no such cocktail or tradition exists in Chult and that the rare stones were colored glass. By that point, the con artist Gannis had already fled to Baldur's Gate with the specter of a kenku assassin's black wing at his back.

## SERVES 2

| | | |
|---|---|---|
| ROUGHLY CRACKED OR SMALL ICE CUBES | 1 OUNCE FALERNUM | ⅓ CUP FRESH PASSION FRUIT PULP (SEE COOK'S NOTE) |
| 1 OUNCE BLUE CURAÇAO | 2 OUNCES FRESH LEMON JUICE | |
| 2 OUNCES DARK RUM | 3 OUNCES PINEAPPLE JUICE | MINT, FOR GARNISH |
| 1 OUNCE LIGHT RUM | 2 OUNCES FRESH ORANGE JUICE | BASIL, FOR GARNISH |

Fill a serving bowl or other large drinking vessel three-quarters of the way full with ice. Add the blue curaçao, dark rum, light rum, falernum, lemon juice, pineapple juice, orange juice, and passion fruit to the bowl and stir to combine. Garnish with mint and basil. Serve at once in rocks glasses.

COOK'S NOTE If you can't find fresh passion fruit at your local market, look for frozen passion fruit pulp with seeds.

# CAPTAIN'S FANCY

L araelra Thundreth is a widely respected wizard in Baldur's Gate; she's considerate of her staff, respectful of her patrons, and dedicated in her study of magic. She often leaves the care of the bar to her employees and retires to her quarters in the late evening to absorb herself in her books.

If there is no trouble to attend to, Laraelra will not emerge until morning, but she will sometimes send out her familiar, a robust scuttling crab, to bring her a sandwich, which the kenku bartenders will delicately balance on the creature's carapace.

When she's in a good mood, Laraelra will also order a hot buttered rum with whipped cream and cinnamon, an indulgent treat that does not match her serious reputation. The Captain pretends to have few vices, but this is among her greatest. The drink is not on the menu, but those in the know can order it by asking for Captain's Fancy.

## SERVES 2

**CINNAMON WHIPPED CREAM**

½ CUP HEAVY CREAM

1 TABLESPOON CONFECTIONERS' SUGAR

⅛ TEASPOON GROUND CINNAMON

2 TABLESPOONS UNSALTED BUTTER

2 TEASPOONS PACKED BROWN SUGAR

¼ TEASPOON GROUND CINNAMON

⅛ TEASPOON GROUND ALLSPICE

⅛ TEASPOON PURE VANILLA EXTRACT

½ CUP DARK RUM

1¼ CUPS HOT WATER

*To make the cinnamon whipped cream:* In a chilled bowl, use an electric hand mixer or whisk to beat the heavy cream until just beginning to thicken. Add the confectioners' sugar and cinnamon. Continue to whip the cream until soft peaks form and the texture is silky. Chill until ready to use, no more than 2 hours.

In a small saucepan, melt the butter over medium heat, stirring frequently until aromatic and slightly browned, about 3 minutes. Stir in the brown sugar, cinnamon, allspice, vanilla, dark rum, and hot water. Remove from the heat. Carefully divide the mixture evenly between heatproof glass mugs. Top with a dollop of whipped cream and serve at once.

# FAERIE FIRE

Many old sea dogs will tell you that Faerie Fire is a preposterous drink, with all its froufrou juices and fancy adornments like popping candy and edible pearls, all of which serve to create a ridiculous sensory experience. But that won't stop them from moseying up to a table of strangers who have ordered a pitcher of Faerie Fire with an offer to exchange seafaring tales for a wee cup of grog. There is more than enough rum in Faerie Fire to overcome their objections!

This drink is named for a simple spell that creates radiant light around every person and object in a small space. Bar staff who can perform the spell will often do so to accompany the drink, usually in celebration of someone's birthday or their victorious return from an adventure. There is even a terrible song that goes with it: "Faerie fire for thee, faerie fire for thee, faerie fire for (name of recipient), faerie fire for thee." The Captain has absolutely forbidden the use of the spell and the singing of the song in her establishment.

## SERVES 6 TO 8

| | | |
|---|---|---|
| SIMPLE SYRUP | 6 OUNCES FALERNUM | ½ TEASPOON EDIBLE GLITTER |
| ½ CUP WATER | 3 OUNCES FRESH LEMON JUICE | POP ROCKS, FOR RIMMING GLASSES |
| ½ CUP SUGAR | 3 OUNCES FRESH ORANGE JUICE | |
| | 6 OUNCES PINEAPPLE JUICE | LEMON WEDGE, FOR RIMMING THE GLASS |
| LARGE ICE CUBES | 12 OUNCES HIBISCUS TEA, COOLED TO ROOM TEMPERATURE | POPPING BOBA |
| 6 OUNCES WHITE RUM | | |
| 3 OUNCES DARK RUM | | ROCK CANDY, FOR GARNISH |

*To make the simple syrup:* In a small saucepan over medium-high heat, add the water and sugar. Bring to a boil, then lower heat to low. Simmer for 5 minutes, stirring occasionally until slightly thickened. Remove from heat. Let fully cool before using. Store any remaining simple syrup in an airtight jar in the refrigerator for up to 2 weeks.

Fill a punch bowl or large pitcher halfway with large ice cubes. Add the white rum, dark rum, falernum, lemon juice, orange juice, pineapple juice, hibiscus tea, 3 ounces of simple syrup, and edible glitter to the punch bowl and mix well with a long-handled spoon. Empty a packet of pop rocks onto a small rimmed plate. Lightly run the cut side of a lemon wedge around the rim of a rocks or stemless wine glass and dip the rim into the pop rocks. To serve, add a spoonful or two of popping boba to each glass and top with punch. Garnish each drink with a stick of rock candy and serve at once.

# ELDRITCH STORM

The bouncers at the Low Lantern are brawny former sailors of the Captain's acquaintance—tall, imposing, and able to tie troublemakers in knots. Their main function is to be silently intimidating to prevent any troublemaking before it happens. The people that guests really must be wary of are the bartenders. All the Captain's bartenders are kenku. These raven-black birdlike people seem more unsettling than threatening. Most patrons barely look at them twice. However, anyone who knows history knows that the first kenku came to Faerûn as assassins, and though most kenku pursue other professions, the Captain's kenku are certainly members of that sinister order, able to quietly and quickly remove any serious "problems" from the bar.

This strange, slightly savory cocktail is a favorite of the kenku; it's dark, elegant, and sinister. As long as the Low Lantern remains, this drink will be on the menu.

## SERVES 2

| MISO-WASHED RUM | ROUGHLY CRACKED OR SMALL ICE CUBES | 1 OUNCE FRESH LIME JUICE |
|---|---|---|
| 3 TABLESPOONS UNSALTED BUTTER | 1 OUNCE COFFEE LIQUEUR | 2 LIME WHEELS, FOR GARNISH |
| ½ TABLESPOON MISO PASTE | 8 OUNCES GINGER BEER | 2 SLICES GINGER, FOR GARNISH |
| 1 CUP DARK RUM | | |

*To make the miso-washed rum:* In a small saucepan over medium heat, melt the butter for about 5 minutes, stirring frequently until aromatic and slightly browned. Remove from the heat and stir in the miso paste until fully combined. Add the rum and allow to cool. Then transfer to a jar and shake well. Refrigerate until the butter is solidified, 1 to 2 hours. Line a fine-mesh strainer with cheesecloth or paper towel, set it over a cup with a spout, and strain the butter solids from the rum.

Fill two highball glasses with ice. Divide the coffee liqueur evenly between the glasses. Slowly add half the ginger beer and lime juice to each glass. Carefully top each cocktail with half of the miso-washed rum. The finished drink should have three visible layers. Garnish with a lime wheel and a slice of ginger. Serve at once.

COOK'S NOTE The type of miso you choose will make a big impact on the flavor imparted on the rum. White miso will yield the sweetest and mildest result, yellow and red lend a more savory profile with faint sweetness, and brown will be the most pungent with intense saltiness.

# RUMTACK

T ack, or cabin bread, is a food that's bitterly familiar to sailors; they're dense, hard, flavorless crackers made with just water and flour. It is miserable to eat and has very few nutrients, but it packs a lot of calories and can last for months, possibly even years. Tack is part of every sailor's rations. The lucky ones also have rum, and soaking a hard biscuit in rum can make it a lot more pleasant to eat and a lot easier to swallow.

Rumtack at the Low Lantern is a significant upgrade to a rum-soaked tack. Inspired by traditional black cake from the islands, this rich, boozy offering is one of the only food items available at the Lantern, and a good ship's captain will often order rumtack for the whole crew to help chase away the haunting memories of long months gumming at horrible crackers.

## SERVES 10 TO 12

**CAKE**

2½ CUPS ALL-PURPOSE FLOUR

2 TEASPOONS BAKING SODA

1 TEASPOON KOSHER SALT

10 TABLESPOONS
UNSALTED BUTTER

½ CUP GINGER BEER

¾ CUP DUTCH-PROCESSED
COCOA POWDER

2 CUPS GRANULATED SUGAR

½ TABLESPOON GROUND
CINNAMON

½ TEASPOON GROUND
ALLSPICE

½ TEASPOON GROUND
CARDAMOM

¼ TEASPOON GROUND
CLOVES

¼ TEASPOON GROUND
GINGER

¼ TEASPOON GROUND
NUTMEG

½ CUP DARK SPICED RUM

1 TABLESPOON PURE
VANILLA EXTRACT

½ CUP BUTTERMILK

2 LARGE EGGS

**GLAZE**

½ CUP UNSALTED BUTTER

¾ CUP PACKED DARK
BROWN SUGAR

¾ CUP DARK SPICED RUM

With a rack in the middle position, preheat the oven to 350°F. Spray a 10- to 12-cup Bundt pan with nonstick cooking spray and dust generously with flour.

*To make the cake:* In a large bowl, whisk together the flour, baking soda, and salt and set aside.

In a large saucepan over medium heat, warm the butter and the ginger beer for 3 to 5 minutes, until the butter is melted. Remove from the heat and add the cocoa powder, sugar, cinnamon, allspice, cardamom, cloves, ginger, and nutmeg. Stir to combine. Add the rum, vanilla, buttermilk, and eggs and stir until the eggs are fully incorporated. Carefully add the butter mixture to the flour mixture and stir well with a rubber spatula until no flour streaks remain.

Pour the batter into the prepared Bundt pan. Bake until a cake tester or toothpick inserted in the thickest part of the cake is removed with a few moist crumbs, 50 to 60 minutes.

*To make the glaze:* In a small saucepan, combine the butter, sugar, and rum. Set the saucepan over medium-high heat, stirring occasionally until the mixture comes to a boil. Reduce the heat to low and simmer for 5 minutes, until slightly thickened and glossy. Remove from the heat.

Remove the cake from the oven and transfer to a wire rack. Using a skewer, poke holes all over the cake, stopping three-quarters of the way into the cake's interior. Spoon half of the glaze over the holes and cool for 30 minutes. Spoon another quarter of the glaze over the cake and let soak for another 30 minutes. Place a serving plate on top of the Bundt pan and invert to turn the cake out, tapping the sides of the pan if necessary to release the cake. Warm the glaze over low heat if necessary to loosen it up and brush the remaining glaze over the top of the cake. Slice and serve. Store the cake covered in the refrigerator for up to 1 week.

# TEQUILA FROM
# THE HALFWAY INN
# NEAR EVERESKA

The Halfway Inn is as close as some travelers may get to the hidden and secretive city of Evereska. This sturdy brick inn is also a trading post where hunters, trappers, prospectors, and farmers from across the region meet to exchange goods and share stories. The patrons include a few skilled artisans from Evereska itself who come here to sell their wares.

As one of the closest taverns to the great desert sands of Anauroch, the Halfway Inn does an excellent trade in tequila, a spirit distilled from the desert cactus—also known in the Elven tongue as "Elquesstria."

WILD-FORAGED
ANAUROCH AGAVE

TEQUILA

SPECIALLY BOTTLED FOR

THE HALFWAY INN

# MOONRISE

The redoubtable elven settlement of Evereska maintains a cool relationship with the Halfway Inn's proprietor, Myrin Silverspear. Silverspear offers a warm welcome to all who step through the doors of his inn, in stark contrast to the proudly unapproachable Evereskans.

In spite of this difference in approach, Evereska tolerates the inn's unusual proximity to the secretive community because the people of Evereska respect Silverspear as a fair broker and because Evereska benefits from having a trading post nearby. It is rumored that Silverspear is an exiled noble of Evereska, which would explain why he is so respected and tolerated and yet still excluded.

The Moonrise cocktail, with its distinct layers, is said to evoke the view of the rising moon from the heightened vantage of Evereska through the haze of the city's own magic field. It's one of the most beautiful and cherished sights and one that Silverspear knows he will never see again.

## SERVES 2

| | | |
|---|---|---|
| 8 BLACKBERRIES | ½ OUNCE GRENADINE | 4 OUNCES TEQUILA |
| 8 OUNCES LEMONADE | 3 DROPS BLACK FOOD COLORING | 4 BLACKBERRIES, FOR GARNISH |
| ROUGHLY CRACKED OR SMALL ICE CUBES | 1 OUNCE COCONUT CREAM LIQUEUR | |

Place the blackberries in a mixing glass or 2-cup measuring cup and use a muddler to break them down completely. Add the lemonade and stir to combine. Pour the mixture through a fine-mesh strainer set over another mixing glass to remove the solids and set aside.

Fill two highball glasses three-quarters of the way full with ice. In a small cup, stir together the grenadine and black food coloring. Divide the mixture evenly between the two glasses. Slowly pour half of the coconut cream liqueur in each glass, being careful to keep the layers separate. Slowly pour half the blackberry lemonade into each glass to create a third layer. Top each cocktail with 2 ounces of tequila and garnish with 2 blackberries. Serve at once.

COOK'S NOTE Creating distinct layers in a cocktail is all dependent on the density of liquids being used to craft the drink. Syrups and liqueurs with a high sugar content will sink to the bottom of the glass, while pure, higher-alcohol spirits float easily on top.

# EYE OF THE BEHOLDER

Contrary to common claim, there is no beauty in the eye of a Beholder. Those dungeon-dwelling creatures are ugly and repugnant floating abominations, with a disturbing number of needle-sharp teeth and ten grotesque eyes on serpentine stalks, all writhing around its one central dinnerplate-size eye. Beholders can kill with a single glance, so they are no laughing matter. However, few people will ever encounter a Beholder, and fewer still will live to tell the tale, so the creatures retain an almost mythic reputation in the minds of many adventurers.

It is with utmost unseriousness that Beholders have been immortalized in the name and design of a tart green party punch. A few glasses of this, and everything seems beautiful in the eye of the beholder.

## SERVES 6 TO 8

| | | |
|---|---|---|
| LYCHEE ICE RING | 3 OUNCES MELON LIQUEUR, SUCH AS MIDORI | ¾ CUP FRESH ACID-ADJUSTED ORANGE JUICE |
| 2 CANS LYCHEE FRUIT AND LIQUID | 1½ CUPS TEQUILA | 3 OUNCES AGAVE NECTAR |
| WATER | 3 OUNCES ORANGE LIQUEUR, SUCH AS TRIPLE SEC OR COINTREAU | 1½ CUPS CLUB SODA |
| ACID-ADJUSTED ORANGE JUICE | | 1 ORANGE WHEEL, FOR GARNISH |
| 1½ TEASPOONS CITRIC ACID | ¾ CUP LYCHEE LIQUID | 1 BLACKBERRY, FOR GARNISH |
| ¾ CUP FRESH ORANGE JUICE | ¾ CUP FRESH LIME JUICE | ROUGHLY CRACKED OR SMALL ICE CUBES, TO SERVE |

*To make the lychee ice ring:* Set aside ¾ cup of the liquid in the lychee cans for the punch. In a large Bundt pan, combine the lychee fruit and remaining liquid. Fill the cake pan with water until the fruit is nearly submerged. Stir and arrange the fruit as desired. Freeze for several hours until the liquid is completely solid. To remove from the mold, dip the pan into warm water for a few seconds to loosen. Invert the pan onto a clean surface and gently tap the sides of the pan until the ice ring slides out. Place the ice ring in a punch bowl and set aside.

*To make the lychee ice ring:* In a small bowl, combine the citric acid with the orange juice and stir until fully dissolved. Set aside.

In the punch bowl, combine the melon liqueur, tequila, orange liqueur, reserved lychee liquid, lime juice, acid-adjusted orange juice, and agave nectar. Stir with a long-handled spoon. Top with club soda, add the ice, and stir gently. Set the slice of orange in the middle of the lychee ice ring with a blackberry on top. Fill as many highball glasses as needed with ice. Serve at once.

# DEADWINTER FIRE

Travelers to the Halfway Inn sometimes bring their traditions and rituals with them. For example, orcish migrants from the rugged lands of Chessenta brought Deadwinter, a festival that marks the turn in midwinter from longer nights to longer days. Deadwinter is a three-day celebration of love for the lost; it's not a sad occasion but rather a joyous one marked with music, laughter, and delicious decorated cakes. Deadwinter Fire is a seasonal specialty, cold on the lips and hot in the belly, with pepper syrup that represents life, love, and passion. This is not a solemn drink; it's spicy!

Competitive celebrants sometimes try to outdo each other with just how much heat they are willing to add to their Deadwinter Fire. First-timers are advised to approach with modesty!

## SERVES 2

**HABANERO LIME SYRUP**

½ CUP WATER

½ CUP SUGAR

1 HABANERO PEPPER, SEEDED, HALVED LENGTHWISE

ZEST OF 1 LIME

ROUGHLY CRACKED OR SMALL ICE CUBES

½ OUNCE FRESH LIME JUICE

6 OUNCES FRESH RUBY RED GRAPEFRUIT JUICE, PLUS 2 SLICES FOR GARNISH

4 OUNCES TEQUILA OR MEZCAL

SODA WATER, TO TOP

*To make the habanero-lime syrup:* In a small saucepan, combine the water and sugar. Bring to a boil over medium-high heat. Add the habanero and lime zest, turn down the heat to low, and simmer for 5 minutes. Remove from the heat and cool for 10 minutes. Strain the mixture into a fine-mesh strainer over a cup with a spout to remove the solids and set aside. Store any remaining habanero syrup in an airtight jar in the refrigerator for up to 1 week.

Fill two highball glasses three-quarters full with ice. Divide the lime juice, 1 ounce of the habanero lime syrup, grapefruit juice, and tequila evenly between the two glasses. Top each with soda water and stir gently to combine. Make a 2-inch slit toward the center point of the grapefruit wheel and slide it onto the rim of each glass. Serve at once.

COOK'S NOTE Use disposable gloves when seeding the habanero to ensure that none of its fiery potency lingers on your fingers!

# SEAFOAM

Sea elves, merfolk, and members of other oceanic cultures are not a common sight in surface-world bars because alcohol is dehydrating, and so is being out of the water. Seafolk are an especially rare sight at the Halfway Inn, which is far from any saltwater coastline. Ocean merchants can find many other places to trade that are not on the edge of a large, dry desert.

Even so, everyone is welcome at the inn, and all staff are trained on how to make this cocktail just in case the occasion demands. Brackish and savory, the Seafoam is undeniably unique, and it has proved popular not just with those rare few seafolk visiting the interior of Faerûn, but with all sorts of landlubbers with a nostalgic fondness for the sea!

## SERVES 2

**NORI SALINE SOLUTION**

¼ CUP WATER

½ TABLESPOON KOSHER SALT

½ SHEET NORI, CUT INTO 1-INCH PIECES

ROUGHLY CRACKED OR SMALL ICE CUBES

4 OUNCES BLANCO TEQUILA

1 OUNCE FRESH LIME JUICE

8 OUNCES SPARKLING MINERAL WATER

¼ SHEET NORI, CUT INTO 2 PIECES ON THE BIAS

*To make the nori saline solution:* In a small saucepan, bring the water and salt to a boil over medium-high heat and stir until the salt is completely dissolved. Remove from the heat. Add the nori pieces and stir to submerge. Allow to steep for 30 minutes to an hour. Strain the mixture into a fine-mesh strainer over a cup with a spout to remove the solids and set aside. Store any remaining saline in an airtight jar in the refrigerator for up to 1 month.

Fill two highball glasses three-quarters full with ice. Divide the tequila, lime juice, and sparkling water evenly between the two glasses. Add ¼ teaspoon of the nori saline solution to each glass and gently stir to combine. Garnish with a triangle of nori and serve at once.

COOK'S NOTE  A simple saline solution can bump up the flavors of any cocktail. Omit the nori, store in a bottle with a glass dropper, and keep on hand for whenever you feel like experimenting. A few drops are enough to make a big impact on any drink.

# POETESS

Many centuries ago, a beautiful young woman with a five-stringed harp of green vines stepped into the roar of a powerful river. She spoke in such elegant tones of the destructive and creative power of nature that the waters calmed around her. As she plucked her strings and continued her recital, she stirred magic into the very rocks of the canyon. This is how Evereska was formed—at least according to one telling.

The woman, an elven goddess known as the Poetess, was either a female aspect or an avatar of Milil, the Faerûn god of creativity. In honor of the Poetess's legacy, bards meet every year at the Halfway Inn for a tournament of battle poetry, an extraordinary event that combines magic, dance, martial arts, and spitting bars.

The official drink of the festival, the Poetess, is as beautiful, elegant, and quietly formidable as the goddess herself.

### SERVES 2

**LAVENDER SYRUP**

½ CUP WATER

½ CUP SUGAR

2½ TABLESPOONS DRIED CULINARY LAVENDER

1 TEASPOON HOT WATER

½ TEASPOON BUTTERFLY PEA POWDER

3 OUNCES BLANCO TEQUILA

1½ OUNCES WHITE VERMOUTH

ROUGHLY CRACKED OR SMALL ICE CUBES

LARGE ICE CUBES

½ OUNCE FRESH LEMON JUICE

2 SPRIGS LAVENDER, FOR GARNISH

LEMON PEEL, FOR GARNISH

*To make the lavender syrup:* In a small saucepan, combine the water and sugar. Bring to a boil over medium-high heat, add the lavender, and stir to combine. Remove from the heat and let steep for 5 minutes. Strain the mixture into a fine-mesh strainer or cheesecloth over a cup with a spout to remove the solids and set aside. In a separate cup, stir together the hot water and butterfly pea powder until no clumps remain. Add to the lavender syrup and mix well. Allow to fully cool before using. Store any remaining lavender syrup in an airtight jar in the refrigerator for up to 1 week.

In a mixing glass, add the tequila, vermouth, and ½ ounce of lavender syrup. Fill the glass halfway with ice and stir with a long-handled spoon to chill, about 30 seconds. Add a large ice cube to two rocks glasses. Strain and divide the mixture evenly between the two glasses. Top with lemon juice, lavender sprigs, and lemon peel. Watch the color change with the addition of acid, and serve at once.

# HELLISH REBUKE

The Halfway Inn tries to offer something for everyone: fine wines for elves from Evereska, frothy ale for dwarves from the mountains, and sweet mead for humans from the prairies. The inn even has a drink concocted specifically for tieflings: a smoky, fiery drink named after a tiefling fire spell.

The reaction was mixed. Proprietor Myrin Silverspear realized that tieflings all had wildly different tastes, no matter what shared culture they have developed. This epiphany was a turning point for the Halfway Inn. Silverspear encouraged his servers to engage with their customers to find out what they really wanted. The staff discovered that some elves actually preferred ale to wine, and some dwarves preferred wine to ale—and some folks from every species and culture enjoyed the punchy kick of a Hellish Rebuke.

## SERVES 2

| CHARRED JALAPEÑO TEQUILA | 1 OUNCE ORANGE LIQUEUR, SUCH AS TRIPLE SEC OR COINTREAU | CHILI-LIME SALT, SUCH AS TAJÍN, FOR GARNISH |
|---|---|---|
| 4 JALAPEÑO PEPPERS | 2 OUNCES FRESH LIME JUICE | LIME WEDGE |
| 750 ML BOTTLE BLANCO TEQUILA | 1 OUNCE AGAVE NECTAR | 2 LIME WHEELS FOR GARNISH |
| | ROUGHLY CRACKED OR SMALL ICE CUBES | 2 JALAPEÑO SLICES, FOR GARNISH |

With a rack in the upper position about 6 inches from the heating element, preheat the broiler on high for 10 minutes. Line a baking sheet with foil.

Place the jalapeños on the prepared baking sheet and roast for 3 to 5 minutes on both sides, until the skin is well charred. Remove from the oven and cool. Slice the stem end from the peppers and halve them lengthwise. Use the back of a knife to rub and remove the charred skin from the jalapeños. Halve them lengthwise once more to form spears and add them to a bottle of tequila. Shake well. Check on the infusion hourly until the desired flavor and heat level are reached, 1 to 3 hours. Remove the jalapeños and store the tequila in a cool, dry place for up to 6 months.

In a cocktail shaker, combine 4 ounces of the charred jalapeño tequila, the orange liqueur, lime juice, and agave nectar. Fill the shaker halfway with ice, cover, and shake to chill, about 30 seconds. Sprinkle chili-lime salt onto a small plate. Gently rub a lime wedge around the rim of two rocks glasses and dip the rims into the chili-lime salt. Fill the glasses three-quarters of the way full with ice. Strain and divide the mixture evenly between the two glasses. Garnish with the lime wheel and jalapeño slice. Serve at once.

# THE HOARD

Every adventurer dreams of discovering a dragon's hoard—the astonishing mound of jewels and riches that are a dragon's most prized possession. Every adventurer also has nightmares about encountering a dragon, which is unfortunate, as dragons are often found asleep on top of their hoard.

The hoard on offer at the Halfway Inn is much easier to enjoy and requires no dragon-taming! Look no further for a platter of crunchy corn chips stacked high with delicious treasures and smothered with golden cheese. Adventure parties often come to blows when splitting the haul from a dragon's hoard. Parties splitting the hoard at the Halfway Inn tend to be less aggressive, though that's not to say that axes have never been thrown and fireballs have never been flung over the last scoop of beans.

---

**SERVES 6 TO 8**

### PICO DE GALLO

¾ POUND RIPE TOMATOES, CUT INTO ¼-INCH DICE

½ TEASPOON KOSHER SALT

1 SMALL WHITE ONION, FINELY DICED, ABOUT ⅓ CUP

1 SMALL SERRANO OR JALAPEÑO PEPPER, FINELY DICED

¼ CUP FINELY CHOPPED FRESH CILANTRO LEAVES

1 TABLESPOON FRESH LIME JUICE

### CHEESE SAUCE

8 OUNCES MONTEREY JACK, CHEDDAR, OR PEPPER JACK CHEESE (OR A COMBINATION), GRATED

1 TABLESPOON CORNSTARCH

1 CUP EVAPORATED MILK, PLUS EXTRA, IF NEEDED

¼ TEASPOON KOSHER SALT

¼ TEASPOON GROUND BLACK PEPPER

¼ TEASPOON GARLIC POWDER

½ TEASPOON CHILI POWDER

½ TEASPOON GROUND CUMIN

2 TABLESPOONS CHOPPED PICKLED JALAPEÑO

2 TEASPOONS HOT SAUCE (OPTIONAL)

### [Assembly]

1 (12-OUNCE) BAG TORTILLA CHIPS, PREFERABLY THICK-CUT OR RESTAURANT-STYLE

1 CUP CANNED BLACK OR PINTO BEANS, DRAINED AND RINSED

½ CUP SLICED PICKLED JALAPEÑOS (OPTIONAL)

8 OUNCES CHEDDAR AND/ OR MONTEREY JACK CHEESE, GRATED

2 AVOCADOS, MASHED

1 TABLESPOON FRESH LIME JUICE

½ TEASPOON KOSHER SALT

¼ CUP COTIJA CHEESE, CRUMBLED

½ CUP SOUR CREAM

1 LARGE RADISH, THINLY SLICED

¼ CUP FRESH CILANTRO LEAVES, ROUGHLY CHOPPED

---

*To make the pico de gallo:* In a medium bowl, sprinkle the tomatoes with salt and toss to combine. Transfer to a fine-mesh strainer, set the strainer over the medium bowl, and allow to drain for 30 minutes. Discard the liquid from the bowl and return the tomatoes to the bowl. Add the onion, serrano, cilantro, and lime juice. Toss to combine, seasoning with more salt to taste. Cover and place in the refrigerator until ready to use.

*To make the cheese sauce:* In a medium saucepan, combine the cheese and cornstarch by tossing them together. Add the evaporated milk and set the saucepan over low heat, stirring constantly until the cheese has melted and the mixture is thickened and bubbly, about 5 minutes. Stir in the salt, pepper, garlic powder, chili powder, cumin, chopped pickled jalapeños, and hot sauce (if using). If the texture is too thick for your liking, thin the cheese sauce with additional evaporated milk. Set aside.

With a rack in the middle position, preheat the oven to 375°F. Line a baking sheet with foil.

*To make the nachos:* Spread half the tortilla chips over the prepared baking sheet and drizzle with half of the cheese sauce. Spread half the beans and jalapeños (if using) evenly over the cheese sauce. Sprinkle half of the grated cheese evenly. Add the remaining chips to create a second layer and repeat the process with the cheese sauce, beans, jalapeños, and grated cheese. Bake for 5 minutes, until the cheese is melted.

While the nachos are baking, in a small bowl, mix to combine the mashed avocado, lime juice, and salt. Remove the nachos from the oven and top with the pico de gallo and cotija cheese. Dollop all over with the avocado mixture and sour cream. Garnish with radish slices and cilantro. Serve at once.

# BRANDY FROM THE DRIFTWOOD TAVERN IN NEVERWINTER

The Driftwood Tavern is an upmarket inn with a fine reputation and a magnificently curated museum recounting Neverwinter's troubled history, which includes sieges, coups, civil uprisings, and the devastating eruption of Mount Hotenow. Exhibits at the museum include graffitied stones from the old city walls, tattered banners from the ruins of Castle Never, and a partly melted city hall clock stalled at the moment of the Hotenow eruption. The tavern has weathered so many catastrophes that it's earned a reputation as a serene oasis in a world of violent change.

The owner, Madame Rosene, is fond of brandy and is sometimes seen putting the world to rights with old friends over a few brandy cocktails. Her patrons try to emulate her refined tastes, which ensures that her cocktails always sell well at the bar!

The
DRIFTWOOD
⚜ TAVERN ⚜

Fine Heirloom Fruit
BRANDY
Aged on Premises in Thundertree Oak Casks

# BRANDY CASSALANTER

The Cassalanter family of Waterdeep exerts a strong influence across the Sword Coast due to their heavy involvement in the banking sector, but the members of this family are definitely more powerful than popular. Rumors abound of their involvement in shady affairs, with talk of necromancy, vampirism, and tax avoidance. There is even scuttlebutt that the current Lord and Lady Cassalanter, Victorio and Ammalia, sold their own young children's souls to a demonic entity and that their eldest child and heir, Osvaldo, is chained up in the depths of the netherworld.

There was a time not long ago when the Cassalanter name was a proud one; Victorio's father, Caladorn Cassalanter, was revered as a hero across the North, and the family as a whole was loved for its philanthropy. Those are the Cassalanters for whom this refined creamy cocktail is named, not the current batch of psychopaths. Superstitious patrons at the Driftwood may order this drink as a "Caladorn" to avoid invoking the Cassalanter name and its diabolical associations.

### SERVES 2

| | | |
|---|---|---|
| 4 OUNCES BRANDY | 3 OUNCES COCONUT MILK OR CREAM (NOT CREAM OF COCONUT) | 4 DASHES CHOCOLATE BITTERS |
| 1 OUNCE CRÈME DE BANANA | | ROUGHLY CRACKED OR SMALL ICE CUBES |

In a cocktail shaker, combine the brandy, crème de banana, coconut milk, and chocolate bitters. Fill halfway with ice, cover, and shake to chill, about 30 seconds. Strain through a fine-mesh cocktail strainer into 2 cocktail glasses. Serve at once.

COOK'S NOTE Double straining this cocktail removes any additional ice shards that may have made their way through the first strain, assuring a perfectly smooth and creamy result. Hold a fine-mesh cocktail strainer above the serving glass with one hand and pour the liquid through the standard strainer into it, shaking or tapping as needed to allow the drink to flow through.

# MADAME ROSENE'S NIGHTCAP

Madame Rosene is an influential figure in Neverwinter—well connected, well informed, and always invested in the city's success. As proprietor of the Driftwood Tavern and curator of the museum, she has an intimate knowledge of the city's past and present tensions. She also has one other advantage up her sleeve: her cellars.

The Driftwood Tavern is one of the only intact buildings in the city to survive multiple cataclysms, and it has not only preserved the many historic artifacts collected under its roof over the centuries, but also a world-class collection of vintage wines and brandies. Madame Rosene enjoys a glass of that brandy every evening, and to share in her wealth, one must be invited to join her for a nightcap.

The cocktail on the tavern's menu does not use Madame Rosene's private reserve; one would never mix such precious spirits! But it's as close as most patrons will get to the experience of a snifter with the aloof and venerable lady herself, and it is what Madame Rosene will order if she has a second or a third drink.

## SERVES 2

| | | |
|---|---|---|
| 3 OUNCES BRANDY | 1 OUNCE RED VERMOUTH | 2 LEMON PEELS, FOR GARNISH |
| 1 OUNCE AMARO | 4 DASHES AROMATIC BITTERS | |
| | ROUGHLY CRACKED OR SMALL ICE CUBES | |

In a mixing glass, combine the brandy, amaro, vermouth, and bitters. Fill the glass halfway with ice and stir with a long-handled spoon until well chilled, about 30 seconds. Strain and divide the mixture evenly between two coupe glasses. Serve at once.

# ENDURANCE

The history of Neverwinter is tumultuous and chaotic. Other cities have experienced similar levels of pain and devastation, but what makes Neverwinter unusual is that it has survived. Neverwinter has endured riots, fires, plagues, storms, coups, sieges, and a volcanic eruption so devastating that it is recorded in the city's history as the Ruining. That last cataclysm destroyed most of the city, but the city still clawed its way back.

Through it all, the Driftwood Tavern has provided a lasting tabernacle and an oasis of certainty through generations of peril. The Endurance cocktail was added to the tavern's menu as a commemoration of that history and of the tavern's place in it. Light, subtle, and summery, it is by design a hopeful drink.

## SERVES 2

| | | |
|---|---|---|
| 4 TO 6 FRESH MINT LEAVES | 4 OUNCES BRANDY | CLUB SODA, TO TOP |
| 4 STRAWBERRIES, CORED AND QUARTERED | ROUGHLY CRACKED OR SMALL ICE CUBES | 2 FRESH MINT SPRIGS, FOR GARNISH |
| 1 OUNCE SIMPLE SYRUP (PAGE 79) | ½ OUNCE ABSINTHE, TO RINSE | 2 STRAWBERRIES, FOR GARNISH |
| | CRUSHED ICE | |

In a cocktail shaker, muddle the mint leaves and strawberries to gently release their juices. Add the simple syrup and brandy. Fill the shaker halfway with ice, cover, and shake to chill, about 30 seconds. Pour ¼ ounce absinthe into each of two highball glasses and swirl to coat. Pour out the excess. Fill the glasses with crushed ice. Strain and divide the mixture evenly between the two glasses, and top with club soda. Garnish each cocktail with a sprig of mint and a strawberry. Serve at once.

COOK'S NOTE  Make sure not to break down the mint leaves too much as you muddle. This may cause the drink to become astringent and more difficult to strain.

# CRAKANEG

When Mount Hotenow erupted and the Ruining began, the dwarf Ambron Bron recalled his mother yelling at him to save the chickens. Not the gold, not the axes, not even his father's ashes, but the chickens. When they reached safety, his mother explained her reasoning: However bad things seem, you can always crack an egg. When you have chickens, you have good food in an egg—and when the chicken stops laying, you still have food.

Ambron recalled this lesson when his family returned to Neverwinter after the restoration. He took a job at the Driftwood Tavern and introduced a brandy eggnog to the menu in tribute to his mother's wisdom. However, the memory of saving those chickens, depending on them in the months after the Ruining and then eating those friends, haunted Ambron. He eventually gave up consuming all animal products and added an egg-free alternative to the menu, Craknoeg.

=== SERVES 6 TO 8 ===

| | | |
|---|---|---|
| 6 LARGE EGG YOLKS | 2 WHOLE CLOVES | 1 CUP HEAVY CREAM |
| ½ CUP SUGAR | 1 STICK CINNAMON | ½ CUP BRANDY |
| 2 CUPS MILK | 1½ TEASPOONS PURE VANILLA EXTRACT | 1 TEASPOON FRESHLY GRATED NUTMEG, PLUS EXTRA FOR GARNISH |

In a large bowl, beat the egg yolks with a whisk or an electric mixer until they begin to lighten in color and get a little fluffy, 1 to 2 minutes. Slowly add the sugar and continue to beat until fluffy and pale yellow. Set aside.

In a medium saucepan, combine the milk, cloves, cinnamon, and vanilla. Set the saucepan over medium heat, stirring occasionally, until the milk mixture is steaming but not yet simmering or reads 155°F on an instant read thermometer. Remove from heat.

Slowly pour the milk into the egg mixture, whisking constantly to avoid curdling. Transfer the mixture back into the saucepan, set over medium heat, and cook, stirring constantly, until the mixture reaches 160°F, thickens slightly, and coats the back of the spoon, about 5 minutes.

Remove from the heat and stir in the cream. Pour the mixture through a fine-mesh strainer set over a pitcher to remove the cloves and cinnamon stick. Stir in the brandy and nutmeg. Let cool at room temperature for 1 hour. Then cover, transfer to the refrigerator, and chill for at least 1 hour, though the texture and flavor will improve the longer it rests. Serve in old-fashioned glasses garnished with grated nutmeg. Store any remaining mixture in an airtight jar in the refrigerator for up to 1 week.

## VEGAN VARIATION
# CRAKNOEG

### SERVES 6 TO 8

2½ CUPS CASHEW MILK

1½ CUPS COCONUT CREAM

3 DATES, PITTED

1 TABLESPOON MAPLE SYRUP

1 TEASPOON PURE VANILLA EXTRACT

½ TEASPOON GROUND CINNAMON

¼ TEASPOON FRESHLY GRATED NUTMEG, PLUS EXTRA FOR GARNISH

¼ TEASPOON GROUND CLOVES

¼ TEASPOON KOSHER SALT

½ CUP BRANDY

In a blender, combine the cashew milk, coconut cream, dates, maple syrup, vanilla, cinnamon, nutmeg, cloves, and salt. Blend on high for 1 to 2 minutes until smooth and creamy. Add the brandy and stir to combine. Transfer the mixture to the refrigerator and chill for at least 1 hour, though flavor will improve the longer it rests. Serve garnished with grated nutmeg. Store any remaining mixture in an airtight jar in the refrigerator for up to 1 week.

# ALMOND BRANDY

The exact recipe for Almond Brandy is a closely guarded secret of the Moonshae Isles. According to one tabaxi thief who came close to stealing the recipe and barely escaped the islands with her life, the fundamentals include sweet almond liqueur blended with strong grape brandy, cut with a little lime for sharpness and a dash of bitters for depth.

Given the importance that Madame Rosene places on authenticity for everything in her museum, her adoption of this recipe in the Driftwood Tavern might be an endorsement of its authenticity. It's also quite likely that the drink sells well to tourists and that regulars also enjoy the bittersweet flavor!

## SERVES 2

| 4 OUNCES BRANDY | 1½ OUNCES AMARETTO | 4 DASHES BITTERS |
|---|---|---|
| | 1½ OUNCES FRESH LIME JUICE | |

In a cocktail shaker, combine the brandy, amaretto, lime juice, and bitters. Fill the shaker halfway with ice, cover, and shake until well chilled, about 30 seconds. Strain and divide the mixture evenly between two cocktail glasses. Serve at once.

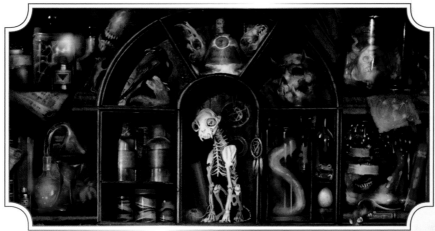

# LITTLEWINTER

As you may have ascertained, it is never winter in Neverwinter. However, magic can be unpredictable and so can weather. On rare occasions, these idiosyncrasies intersect, and it becomes cold enough in the city to maybe wear a coat.

Folks who have adapted to life in cold climates can usually tolerate plummeting temperatures with a shrug, but people living in warm climates seem to notice every drop of one degree on the thermometer. In Neverwinter, as soon as there's a slight chill in the air, residents call it a "littlewinter" and retreat to the tavern to order a hot toddy. This popular variation is so delicious, with its mix of maple syrup, cinnamon, and brandy, that one almost hopes for a little winter to appreciate it!

## SERVES 6 TO 8

| | | |
|---|---|---|
| 4½ CUPS WATER | 1½ OUNCES MAPLE SYRUP | ½ BOSC OR BARTLETT PEAR, CUT INTO THIN SLICES (ABOUT 3 SLICES PER GLASS) |
| 9 OUNCES BRANDY | 1½ OUNCES FRESH LEMON JUICE | |
| 3 OUNCES RED VERMOUTH | 8 CINNAMON STICKS, TO GARNISH | |

In a large saucepan, bring the water to a boil over high heat. Remove from the heat and add the brandy, red vermouth, maple syrup, and lemon juice. Stir to combine. Add 1 cinnamon stick and 3 slices of pear to each of the heatproof glass mugs. Ladle punch into the mugs and serve at once.

# HIGH SUN FLORENTINES

The High Sun games are a particularly brutish "sporting" event that have been abolished and revived by successive Lords of Neverwinter across the generations, all depending on the mood of the time and how great a need there is to distract the common folk. The games see teams of adventurers—or prisoners, in most cases—attempting to navigate a shifting maze filled with monsters in a stadium of thousands of cheering fans. The fans are mostly cheering for the monsters.

Naturally, the city's grandees watch the game from more elevated positions, where they are less likely to get splashed by some errant slime. From their lofty boxes, they are served fine wines and lacy little cookies. High Sun Florentines are the absolute height of refinement and as brittle as a barbarian's bones in the jaws of a displacer beast.

## MAKES 24 COOKIES

¾ CUP SUGAR

2 TABLESPOONS HEAVY CREAM

2 TABLESPOONS LIGHT CORN SYRUP OR AGAVE NECTAR

5 TABLESPOONS UNSALTED BUTTER

½ TEASPOON PURE VANILLA EXTRACT

1¾ CUPS BLANCHED SLICED ALMONDS

3 TABLESPOONS ALL-PURPOSE FLOUR

1 TABLESPOON COCOA POWDER

2 TABLESPOONS FINELY GRATED ORANGE ZEST, FROM 1 ORANGE

¼ TEASPOON CAYENNE PEPPER

¼ TEASPOON FINE SALT

4 OUNCES DARK CHOCOLATE, CHOPPED

1 TABLESPOON FLAKE SEA SALT, SUCH AS MALDON

1 TABLESPOON ALEPPO, URFA, OR KOREAN CHILI FLAKES

24 EDIBLE GOLD LEAVES (OPTIONAL)

With a rack in the middle position, preheat the oven to 350°F. Line as many rimmed baking sheets as you need with parchment paper or a silicone baking mat.

In a small saucepan, combine the sugar, cream, corn syrup, and butter. Set over medium heat and cook, stirring occasionally, until the mixture comes to a rolling boil. Continue to boil for 1 minute until the syrup is slightly thickened. Remove from the heat and stir in the vanilla. Set aside.

In the bowl of a food processor, pulse the almonds until very finely chopped. Transfer the chopped almonds to a large bowl. Add the flour, cocoa powder, orange zest, cayenne pepper, and salt, and stir to combine using a rubber spatula. Pour the butter mixture into the almond mixture and stir to combine. Cool for 20 minutes, or until cool enough to handle.

PUNCHEONS & FLAGONS

Use a tablespoon to create balls of dough. Distribute the dough balls evenly on the prepared baking sheets, leaving 3 to 4 inches of space between them, about 6 dough balls per sheet. Bake one pan at a time for 10 to 11 minutes, rotating halfway through baking, until the cookies have spread into a thin layer and are an even golden color. Remove from the oven and allow to cool on the baking sheet for 5 minutes. Use a 3- to 3½-inch round cookie cutter to cut the cookies into neat circles. Transfer to a wire rack to fully cool. Repeat with the remaining dough.

While the cookies are cooling, place the dark chocolate in a heatproof bowl. Microwave for 30 seconds at 50% power, stir, and continue to microwave for 30-second intervals and stir until fully melted and smooth. Using a spoon, drizzle the cookies with the chocolate. You can also dip them in the chocolate and set them back on the baking sheet. Sprinkle with sea salt and chili flakes. Place the cookies in the refrigerator until the chocolate is set, about 10 minutes. Garnish with an edible gold leaf and serve at once.

# EXQUISITE RARITIES
## FROM ONE-EYED JAX
## IN LUSKAN

Situated on the north bank of the Mirar River, One-Eyed Jax has a reputation as a haven for pirates, smugglers, and mercenaries—a reputation shared by the entire town of Luskan. Despite that reputation and a seemingly ramshackle appearance, the Jax is one of the safer places for visitors to Luskan. The bar does not brook trouble, and anyone interfering with business is liable to be thrown into the icy-cold waters of the Mirar. Salt winds sometimes howl through the walls, but under the tattered import labels that paper those walls is a surprisingly robust oak-beamed building. Nothing here is exactly as it appears.

The drinks at the One-Eyed Jax change depending on what can be acquired through fair means or foul. The mixed drinks are made from the types of bottles one would find getting dusty at the back of other bars—and that the owners of other bars might not notice going missing!

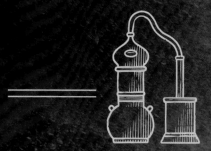

# EXQUISITE RARITY

**NO** **7**

SHREWDLY · PROCURED

*THE*
## ONE-EYED JAX

May contain rice wine,
sugar spirit, apricot kernels,
bitter herbs, citrus, aniseed
or practically anything else.

# GOLDEN WAY

Though Luskan sits at the remote and frigid far north of the Sword Coast, it is a city with a long reach. Its thriving harbor and busy rivers and roads connect it to towns and settlements across the Shining Sea, beyond the sands of Anauroch, and as far away as Kara-Tur. Outsiders say Luskan sits at the edge of the world, but residents of Luskan say that they have the whole of the world on their doorstep.

That Luskan worldliness is evident in the work of tiefling dressmaker Iono Spooner, who sources fabric from all across Toril to create extraordinary costumes for the Luskan traveling carnival, the Sea Maiden's Faire. The carnival brings home beautiful silks, sturdy bamboo fibers, exotic dyes, and rare animal hides, and Iono transforms them all with his clever eye and deft fingers. Iono rarely ventures beyond the walls of his workshop, let alone the walls of his city, but he has been known to make it to the Jax, where he always orders a Golden Way. The drink is named for the largest trade route connecting West to East, and it is an apt celebration of the treasures of trade with flavors not typically native to frigid Luskan!

## SERVES 2

½ CUP DICED CANTALOUPE

3 OUNCES AMBER SAKE
(SEE COOK'S NOTE)

1 OUNCE ORANGE LIQUEUR

1 OUNCE FRESH YUZU OR
LEMON JUICE

½ OUNCE HONEY

ROUGHLY CRACKED OR
SMALL ICE CUBES

In a cocktail shaker, use a muddler to pulverize the cantaloupe until the fruit is lightly mashed and the juices are released. Add the sake, orange liqueur, yuzu juice, and honey to the shaker. Fill the shaker halfway with ice. Cover and shake for 30 seconds to chill. Strain and divide the mixture evenly between two coupe glasses. Serve at once.

COOK'S NOTE  Sweet and rich, amber sake is aged in oak barrels for several years. This process not only deepens the spirit's color but results in a more complex and aromatic expression of the sake with nutty notes of toffee or aged fruit.

# THE BAG

The Bag is a celebration drink for the successful plunderer; it's what a flashy pirate or highway robber orders when they've come into money and want to show off. A thief secures the bag and then a thief enjoys the Bag. This rich, indulgent, creamy drink could send a person to sleep, but the strong coffee in it is meant to counteract those effects, ensuring that the thief is not relieved of his bag before he can enjoy it.

The owner of the One-Eyed Jax, the flamboyant drow swashbuckler Jarlaxle "Jax" Baenre, has a love for the pompous swagger of this drink. It matches his own personality. Jax used charm and wit to place himself in a position of power in Luskan and has found a sort of rhythm in its chaos. He plays the city like a lute. Jax keeps close watch on criminal activities in Luskan through his mercenary band of drow outsiders, the Bregan D'aerthe, and he always knows when and where the power is shifting. Some thieves don't want to signal a successful job by ordering the Bag, so Jax will sometimes send the drink to their table just to make sure they know that they have been noticed.

## SERVES 2

| | | |
|---|---|---|
| 2 OUNCES AMARETTO | 1 OUNCE ESPRESSO, STRONG BREWED COFFEE, OR COLD BREW CONCENTRATE | 1 OUNCE HEAVY CREAM |
| 1 OUNCE PISTACHIO LIQUEUR | | ROUGHLY CRACKED OR SMALL ICE CUBES |
| 1 OUNCE COFFEE LIQUEUR | | |

In a mixing glass, combine the amaretto, pistachio liqueur, coffee liqueur, espresso, and heavy cream. Fill halfway with ice. Using a long-handled spoon, stir well for 30 seconds to chill. Fill two rocks glasses halfway with ice. Strain and divide the mixture evenly between the two glasses. Serve at once.

# NOBLE PRETENDER

**M**any con artists and swindlers pass through Luskan. Those who chance their hand in the wrong venue or move on the wrong mark often don't make it out of the town. One story tells of a man named Gannis Redthumb, a self-proclaimed fugitive aristocrat from Damara seeking safe passage from his persecutors. He plied the patrons of the One-Eyed Jax with fancy drinks and told his new friends that he was carrying magic pits and seeds for winter peaches and strawberries that could grow in bitter snow and feed the hungry through the dead months. Gannis found many potential buyers for his magic fruit—he hooked their interest over strong drinks that loosened their purse strings. Unfortunately for him, the One-Eyed Jax shares some customers with the Low Lantern in Waterdeep. One day, a quiet kenku arrived in town and perched unnoticed in the shadows of the bar. The next day, Gannis was pulled out of the bay in a fishing net.

A drink inspired by Gannis Redthumb's misadventure is still served at the Jax, a reminder to all patrons that the games they play beyond these doors are not tolerated inside them.

### SERVES 2

| | | |
|---|---|---|
| 4 SLICES FROZEN PEACHES | 3 OUNCES AMARETTO | ROUGHLY CRACKED OR SMALL ICE CUBES |
| 2 STRAWBERRIES, HULLED AND QUARTERED | 1½ OUNCES CRANBERRY JUICE | |
| | 1½ OUNCES FRESH LEMON JUICE | |

Fill a cocktail shaker with peaches and strawberries. Using a muddler, break them down until the fruit is lightly mashed and the juices are released Add the amaretto, cranberry juice, and lemon juice. Fill the shaker halfway with ice. Cover and shake for 30 seconds to chill. Fill two rocks glasses halfway with ice. Strain and divide the mixture evenly between the two glasses. Serve at once.

# ELFHARROW KISS

An Elfharrow kiss is not as sweet as it sounds. Elfharrow is a barren desert in Southwest Faerûn; it's hot, dry, and hostile to many forms of life. The lush forest that once filled this land died out when the climate changed, leaving behind a near-dead terrain inhabited by a few tribal communities that fiercely defend their limited resources from intruders. Unwelcome visitors might be greeted by an arrow in the forehead before they even know that they are not alone. That is an Elfharrow kiss.

The bitter smoky cocktail named for that cold welcome is a bit of a history lesson in a glass, with elderflower representing the region's flourishing past and mezcal from desert agave plants representing the prickly present.

## SERVES 2

| | | |
|---|---|---|
| 2 OUNCES MEZCAL | 2 OUNCES FRESH LIME JUICE | ROUGHLY CRACKED OR SMALL ICE CUBES |
| 2 OUNCES CAMPARI | ½ OUNCE SIMPLE SYRUP (PAGE 79) | FRESH OR DRIED EDIBLE FLOWERS, FOR GARNISH |
| 2 OUNCES ELDERFLOWER LIQUEUR | | |

In a cocktail shaker, combine the mezcal, Campari, elderflower liqueur, lime juice, and simple syrup. Fill the shaker halfway with ice. Cover and shake for 30 seconds to chill. Strain and divide the mixture evenly between two coupe or cocktail glasses. Garnish with edible flowers. Serve at once.

COOK'S NOTE Mezcal imparts a distinctive smokiness on this cocktail. The agave used to produce it is cooked in pits before fermentation, resulting in a unique, campfire intensity.

# TYMORA'S COINS

I f the Bag (page 124) is enjoyed by brigands celebrating good fortune after a job, Tymora's Coin is meant to solicit good fortune before a job, usually by a crew of brigands working together. Tymora, the god of luck, is a mercurial and kind figure who is as likely to smile upon a rogue as a paladin so long as they refrain from violence and target the greedy.

The titular coin is Tymora's symbol because sometimes one's fate feels as random as flipping one. The anise and lavender in the punch both carry a blessing for luck, and the lemon wheels represent Tymora's symbol. The number of "coins" that spill from the pitcher into each person's drink represents how much luck the goddess is granting each member of the crew. This can lead to some nervousness if one member of the crew gets no lemons at all.

We leave the reader to speculate what it says about the nature of thieves that the traditional drink before a job is enjoyed by a group and the traditional drink after a job serves only one or two.

## SERVES 6 TO 8

**LAVENDER SYRUP**

½ CUP WATER

½ CUP SUGAR

2½ TABLESPOONS DRIED CULINARY LAVENDER

10 OUNCES FRESH LEMON JUICE (APPROXIMATELY 5 LEMONS)

1 LEMON, SLICED INTO ¼-INCH WHEELS

1½ CUPS OUZO OR OTHER ANISE SPIRIT

ROUGHLY CRACKED OR SMALL ICE CUBES

4 CUPS CLUB SODA OR SPARKLING WATER

LAVENDER SPRIGS, FOR GARNISH

*To make the lavender syrup:* In a small saucepan, combine the water and sugar. Bring to a boil over medium-high heat. Add the lavender and stir to combine. Remove from the heat and let steep for 5 minutes. Set a fine-mesh strainer or cheesecloth over a heatproof container and pour the syrup through to remove the solids. Let cool completely before using.

In a large pitcher, combine the lemon juice, lemon slices, all of the lavender syrup, and ouzo. Fill the pitcher halfway with ice and, using a long-handled spoon, stir for 30 seconds until chilled. Add the club soda and stir gently. Fill as many highball glasses as needed with ice. Garnish with lavender sprigs and serve at once.

COOK'S NOTE It seems almost every culture has their own version of an anise spirit. Most will work in this refreshing lemony punch, provided you select something clear. If you can't find ouzo, keep an eye out for sambuca, arak, raki, mastika, or pastis. For a lower-alcohol-content libation, choose anisette or aguardente; each contains 30% alcohol or less.

# GREENGRASS

When a cold winter ends, and the snow thaws and the icy rivers crack and flow once more, the sun beats down and the first buds of new growth unfurl from the warming soil. It is then people's thoughts often turn to the future, to possibility, and to fertility. Across Faerûn, the coming of spring is marked with a festival called Greengrass. Offerings are made to the gods in hope of a fertile season, and people come together to dance and drink. Spring comes harder and slower to Luskan than in many places, and that makes this bright, verdant herbal cocktail all the more vital. The Greengrass perfectly captures the spirit and mood of the festival all year round.

Greengrass is very popular with those who feel an intense connection to nature, especially the members of the wide-ranging Emerald Enclave, a collective of druids and rangers with agents everywhere. Someone ordering a Greengrass cocktail may be a member of the Enclave signaling their arrival in town to possible friends—or enemies.

## SERVES 2

| | | |
|---|---|---|
| ½ CUP FRESH CILANTRO | ROUGHLY CRACKED OR SMALL ICE CUBES | CLUB SODA OR SPARKLING WATER, FOR TOPPING OFF |
| 2 LIMES, CUT INTO WEDGES | 3 OUNCES CACHACA | |
| 4 TEASPOONS SUGAR | 1 OUNCE FALERNUM | |

In the bottom of each of two highball glasses, place half of the cilantro and half of the limes. Add 2 teaspoons of sugar to each glass. Using a muddler, work the sugar into the limes and cilantro until the juices and aromas are released. Fill the glasses three-quarters of the way with ice. Divide the cachaca and falernum evenly between the two glasses. Top each glass with soda water and stir gently to combine. Serve at once.

COOK'S NOTE Cachaca is known for its distinctive grassy and vegetal flavor profile. Though somewhat similar in taste to light rum, cachaca can only be produced from fermented sugarcane juice; rum often uses sugarcane by-products, such as molasses. This results in a greener, grassier finish thatn you wouldn't typically find in its counterpart.

# SCRAP AND OIL

O n a bountiful day, the One-Eyed Jax has fish a-plenty to fry and serve
its guests. In leaner times, the bar sometimes turns to other methods
to feed the hungry. According to rumor, "scrap and oil" was originally made
using food waste plundered from the alleys behind Luskan's more respectable
establishments or from the scraps that wealthy homes set aside to feed
their pigs. The cook at the Jax believed that his drunken customers would
eat anything placed in front of them if it came battered and deep fried with
a dipping sauce, and he was absolutely correct. In fact, the dish proved so
popular that it was added to the menu.

Supposedly the bar now uses its own fresh leftovers to create these tasty
fritters, and if you believe that, there's a man in the back room of the bar who
would like to sell you a magic chicken.

## SERVES 4 TO 6

| DIPPING SAUCE | | |
| --- | --- | --- |
| ½ CUP PLAIN GREEK YOGURT | ½ CUP CHICKPEA FLOUR | 1 CLOVE GARLIC, MINCED |
| 1 TABLESPOON FINELY CHOPPED FRESH HERBS, SUCH AS CILANTRO, MINT, OR DILL | 2 TABLESPOONS RICE FLOUR | ¼ TEASPOON GROUND CUMIN |
| | ½ TEASPOON BAKING POWDER | ½ TEASPOON GROUND CORIANDER |
| 1 TABLESPOON FRESH LEMON JUICE | 1 LARGE EGG | ½ TEASPOON PAPRIKA |
| 1 TEASPOON EXTRA-VIRGIN OLIVE OIL | 2 POUNDS VEGETABLES OF CHOICE, GRATED OR THINLY SLICED (SEE COOK'S NOTE) | ½ TEASPOON KOSHER SALT |
| ¼ TEASPOON KOSHER SALT | 2 TABLESPOONS FINELY CHOPPED FRESH HERBS, SUCH AS CILANTRO, MINT, OR DILL | FRESHLY GROUND BLACK PEPPER, TO TASTE |
| | | OLIVE OR VEGETABLE OIL, FOR FRYING |

In a small bowl, stir together the yogurt, herbs, lemon juice, olive oil, and salt.
Cover and set aside in the refrigerator until ready to serve.

In a medium bowl, whisk to combine the chickpea flour, rice flour, and baking
powder. In a large bowl, whisk the egg until no streaks remain. Squeeze any
excess water out of the wetter vegetables into the sink. To the bowl with the
egg, add the vegetables, garlic, chopped herbs, cumin, coriander, paprika,

salt, and pepper. Sprinkle half of the flour mixture onto the vegetable mixture and combine with a rubber spatula. Test the mixture by forming a few patties in your hands. If they fall apart, sprinkle and mix in more of the flour mixture a tablespoon at a time until the patties hold together.

Line a plate with paper towels. In a large skillet, heat $\frac{1}{8}$ inch of oil over medium-high heat until shimmering. Using a $\frac{1}{4}$-cup measuring cup, scoop the fritter batter into the pan and gently flatten it with a spatula until it's about $\frac{1}{3}$ inch thick. Continue to add batter to the pan, making sure to leave at least 2 inches between the fritters. Fry for 2 to 3 minutes until the fritters are golden on the bottom, then flip and cook for 2 to 3 more minutes on the second side. Transfer the cooked fritters to the paper towel–lined plate. Continue until no batter remains. Serve at once with the prepared dipping sauce.

COOK'S NOTE This recipe is the perfect way to use any leftover vegetables you may have on hand. Ideally, your cut vegetables should all be around the same size. Slice cabbages and onions thinly. Leafy greens like kale or chard work best when blanched, squeezed, and chopped. Grate root vegetables like carrots or sweet potato with the large holes of a box grater. Grate or cut zucchini and other squashes into matchsticks, and make sure to sprinkle them with a few pinches of salt to draw out any moisture. Drain them for at least 30 minutes before patting them dry and adding to your fritter mixture.

# WINE FROM
# THE MOONSTONE MASK
# IN NEVERWINTER

Intrigue is the specialty of the house at the Moonstone Mask, a glitzy and glamorous high-end establishment with lithe, beautiful, attentive servers who always wear masks when they work. These magnetically attractive people are enchanted against mind magic, making them perfect confidantes when the wine is flowing, as any secrets entrusted to them cannot be plucked from their thoughts.

Wine is the other specialty of the Moonstone Mask, which claims to have the best cellars in Faerûn. The establishment's location on a floating rock held in place by chains means it also has the highest cellars in Faerûn.

# WINE

### HAND-SELECTED
### by SOMMELIERS at

## THE

# *Moonstone Mask*

### BOTTLE-AGED
### in the FINEST and HIGHEST
### CELLARS in FAERÛN

# UTMOST DISCRETION

At the Moonstone Mask, "utmost discretion" is both a drink and request, and the establishment prides itself on providing both. This dry, effervescent drink was originally referred to as "the house special," provided to guests freely on arrival as a welcome gesture in the establishment's earliest days. Each guest was greeted by the host with a promise of "utmost discretion" and handed a drink, and the association stuck.

These days, the drink has to be ordered, but patrons are assured that discretion still comes free at the Moonstone Mask.

## SERVES 2

| | | |
|---|---|---|
| 2 TEASPOONS SUGAR | 2 OUNCES FINO SHERRY | PINK TUILE COOKIES, FOR GARNISH (OPTIONAL) |
| 6 DASHES BITTERS | 8 OUNCES SPARKLING WINE, CHILLED | |

In each of two flute glasses, combine 1 teaspoon of sugar, 3 dashes of bitters, and 1 ounce of sherry. Using a long-handled spoon, stir until the sugar has dissolved (see Cook's Note). Add 4 ounces of sparkling wine to each glass. Gently stir to combine. Garnish with a cookie and serve at once.

COOK'S NOTE It's important to get the sugar dissolved into the first addition of liquids. Stirring too aggressively once the sparkling wine has been added can result in a bubbly mess spilling out of your glass!

# LADY OPHALA

One of the remarkable features of the Moonstone Mask is that it sits atop a floating rock anchored to the ground by heavy iron chains. This unusual arrangement was a side effect of the wide-reaching cataclysm of 1385 dubbed the "Spellplague," but the owners of the Mask decided it suited their purposes. Being located on a floating rock both speaks to the elite, elevated character of the venue and makes it much harder for unwelcome guests to intrude.

To mark the venue's centenary, the Lady Ophala cocktail was created. Named for founding proprietor Lady Ophala Cheldarstorn, the luxurious drink is "garnished" with ice cream to evoke the Mask's unusual outward appearance.

## SERVES 2

2 OUNCES CAMPARI OR AMARO

2 OUNCES VERMOUTH

ROUGHLY CRACKED OR SMALL ICE CUBES

4 OUNCES SPARKLING WINE

2 SCOOPS VANILLA ICE CREAM

In a mixing glass, combine the Campari and vermouth. Fill the mixing glass halfway with ice. Using a long-handled spoon, stir for 30 seconds until chilled. Strain and divide the mixture evenly between two coupe glasses. Add 2 ounces of sparkling wine to each glass and stir gently to combine. Top each glass with a scoop of vanilla ice cream.

# FEYWINE PUNCH

Honey-sweet, effervescent, and as floral as a garden on a warm spring day, Feywine has a unique reputation among elves, who associate it almost exclusively with celebrations and victory feasts. Liset Cheldar, the half-elf current proprietor of the Moonstone Mask, stirred controversy when she started serving Feywine to her customers, as the proper recipe for Feywine is not supposed to be shared outside of elven society. A delegation of elven dignitaries descended on the bar to taste her offering and left satisfied, which led many observers to conclude that Liset could not be serving real Feywine but instead a homemade punch "inspired" by the true recipe and not subject to elven prohibitions!

Whether the Feywine at the Mask is made from the breath of moonlight captured in glistening dew on the skin of rare grapes in the Feywild or by mixing strong liquor with fruit juice and sparkling wine, no one can say for sure. Liset's Feywine certainly has the desired effect of the original in making patrons merry!

## SERVES 6 TO 8

½ CUP ELDERFLOWER LIQUEUR

¾ CUP FRESH GRAPEFRUIT JUICE

3 OUNCES FRESH LEMON JUICE

2 OUNCES HONEY

½ TABLESPOON ROSE WATER

ROUGHLY CRACKED OR SMALL ICE CUBES

1 (750 ML) BOTTLE SPARKLING WINE

In a large pitcher, combine the elderflower liqueur, grapefruit juice, lemon juice, honey, and rose water. Using a long-handled spoon, stir until the honey has fully dissolved into the mixture. Fill the pitcher halfway with ice. Add the sparkling wine to the pitcher and gently stir to combine. Serve at once in rocks or stemless wine glasses.

# MANY STARS

The city of Neverwinter has faced its share of power struggles over the years, but the city's history could have turned out very differently. Some of its gravest threats were quietly dealt with by a secretive guild of arcane mages known as the Many Starred Cloak who devote themselves to protecting the city. Rumor has it that one of their members from this forgotten organization was Lady Ophala, who established the Moonstone Mask to fund and support their operations. It's also said that a secret room exists at the establishment where members of the guild once met to make their plans. The name of the guild lives on in this sweet, spiced, delicious wine cocktail that remains popular throughout the blazing Neverwinter summer.

The current owners of the Mask insist that if any secret meeting room ever existed, they have not found it; and if any such guild ever met there, they know nothing about it; and if the guild still exists and is still meeting there, they certainly will not answer questions about it, so perhaps you should order another drink.

=== SERVES 6 TO 8 ===

| | | |
|---|---|---|
| SPICED SYRUP | 1 PEAR, CUT INTO ¼-INCH SLICES | 1 CUP POMEGRANATE JUICE |
| ¼ CUP WATER | | ¼ CUP FRESH ORANGE JUICE |
| ¼ CUP SUGAR | 1 ORANGE, CUT INTO ¼-INCH ROUNDS | 1 OUNCE FRESH LEMON JUICE |
| 1 CINNAMON STICK | ½ CUP POMEGRANATE ARILS | 2 OUNCES BRANDY |
| 1 WHOLE CLOVE | 1 (750 ML) BOTTLE LIGHT-TO MEDIUM-BODIED RED WINE | 2 OUNCES ORANGE LIQUEUR, SUCH AS COINTREAU |
| 1 WHOLE STAR ANISE | | ROSEMARY SPRIGS, TO GARNISH |

*To make the spiced syrup:* In a small saucepan, combine the water and sugar and bring to a boil over medium-high heat. Reduce the heat to low. Add the cinnamon stick, clove, and star anise and let simmer for 5 minutes, until the syrup is slightly thickened. Remove from the heat. Let the syrup fully cool before using. Store any remaining syrup in an airtight jar in the refrigerator for up to 1 week.

In a large pitcher, place the pear slices, orange rounds, and pomegranate arils. Pour ¼ cup of the spiced syrup and whole spices over the fruit and stir gently with a wooden spoon. Add the red wine, fruit juices, brandy, and orange liqueur to the pitcher. Stir with a wooden spoon to combine. Refrigerate for at least 4 hours, preferably overnight. Serve over ice with fruit in each rocks or stemless wine glass and garnish with a sprig of rosemary.

# RIME OF THE FROSTMAIDEN

C old weather is a half-remembered idea for many residents of Neverwinter, where the climate stays warm and balmy year-round thanks to magic intercession. In many parts of Faerûn, for many species, ice presents an existential threat to survival. In Neverwinter, it is a way to cool drinks.

This frozen wine cocktail is named for Auril, a god of winter known for her merciless indifference to living things. It's said the land around her is magically frozen to a degree that far outmatches the trickery that keeps Neverwinter warm. Followers of the Frostmaiden have occasionally protested the inclusion of this drink on the Mask's menu as they see it as a mockery of their god, but Auril has been dormant for generations and her followers are not very powerful. Most crucially, the drink is too delicious to drop from the menu.

### SERVES 6

| | | |
|---|---|---|
| 1 (750 ML) BOTTLE DRY WHITE WINE | ⅓ CUP FROZEN BLUEBERRIES | 1½ OUNCES FRESH LEMON JUICE |
| | 1½ OUNCES BLUE CURAÇAO | 2 TABLESPOONS AGAVE SYRUP |

Pour the bottle of wine into a 13 × 9-inch pan or in two ice cube trays. Place the wine-filled pan into the freezer and let it chill for 6 hours, until mostly solid. Scrape the frozen wine into a blender jar. Add the blueberries, blue curaçao, lemon juice, and agave syrup and blend until smooth. Transfer the blender jar to the freezer to chill for 30 minutes, until the mixture has thickened. Return the blender jar to its base and pulse the mixture a few times to loosen it. Pour into champagne coupes and serve at once.

COOK'S NOTE Using frozen blueberries will help keep your mixture cool despite the heat generated by the blender. It also increases the intensity of the berries' natural coloring.

# BEAUTY MARK

The servers at the Mask have a sterling reputation—they are attentive, intelligent, and graceful. They are also anonymous. Whatever their species, whatever their gender, all servers dress in sheer black and wear bespoke masks to disguise their faces. The servers also wear amulets that protect them from mind-reading and mind-control. All of this anonymity makes these servers appear especially trustworthy to any guests looking for confidantes to speak to or perhaps to spend a few hours with in one of the private rooms.

On one occasion a guest insisted to his friends that he had identified one of the servers by a beauty mark on her neck. When he looked again, the beauty mark had moved to another server, then to all the servers, then to none of them. The Beauty Mark cocktail serves as a gentle reminder to guests that they must respect the servers' privacy just as much as the servers respect theirs.

## SERVES 2

2 TEASPOONS PINK PEPPERCORNS, PLUS ½ TEASPOON FOR GARNISH

4 OUNCES FINO SHERRY

4 OUNCES SWEET VERMOUTH

ROUGHLY CRACKED OR SMALL ICE CUBES

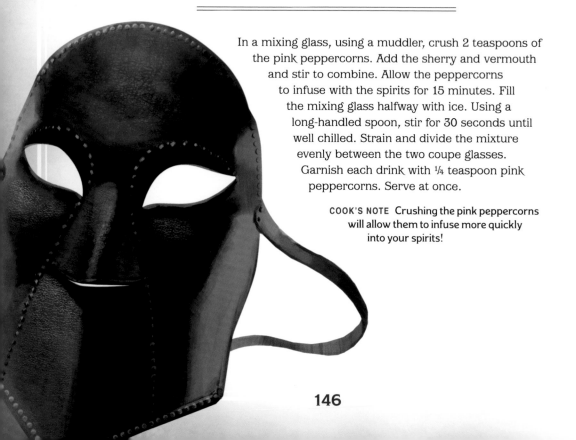

In a mixing glass, using a muddler, crush 2 teaspoons of the pink peppercorns. Add the sherry and vermouth and stir to combine. Allow the peppercorns to infuse with the spirits for 15 minutes. Fill the mixing glass halfway with ice. Using a long-handled spoon, stir for 30 seconds until well chilled. Strain and divide the mixture evenly between the two coupe glasses. Garnish each drink with ¼ teaspoon pink peppercorns. Serve at once.

COOK'S NOTE Crushing the pink peppercorns will allow them to infuse more quickly into your spirits!

146

# COURTESANS

Private rooms are available at the Moonstone Mask, and guests can order food and drink to their room and request a specific server to bring it. One particularly popular order is a serving of courtesans. These sweet roasted figs are a decadent indulgence with a long list of purported benefits that have made them legendary. Figs are said to stir arousal, of course. Pistachios boost one's vigor. Goat's cheese feeds desire, and honey encourages sensuality.

Liset Cheldar makes no specific claims to the aphrodisiac property of this dish, but establishment powerbrokers certainly spend a small fortune testing the possibility.

## SERVES 8

4 OUNCES SOFT GOAT CHEESE

16 FRESH, RIPE FIGS

SEA SALT, TO TASTE

1 TEASPOON PLUS
1 TABLESPOON HONEY

3 TABLESPOONS SHELLED
PISTACHIOS, CHOPPED

FRESHLY CRACKED BLACK
PEPPER, TO TASTE

1 TABLESPOON EXTRA-VIRGIN
OLIVE OIL

In a medium bowl, place the goat cheese and set it aside to bring it up to room temperature, about 1 hour.

Meanwhile, trim the stems from the figs and slice an "X" into the top of each, going about three-quarters of the way through the fig so that the bottom remains intact. Use your index finger to make an indentation in the center of the cut side of the fig to keep the interior of the fruit exposed.

Preheat the oven to 400°F. Line a baking sheet with parchment paper or foil. Arrange the cut figs on the prepared baking sheet and sprinkle each with a pinch of salt.

Once the cheese has softened, add 1 teaspoon of honey and the pistachios to the cheese and stir well with a fork. Add salt and pepper. Stuff each fig with about 1 teaspoon of the goat cheese mixture. Drizzle with olive oil and bake for 5 to 7 minutes, until the cheese looks soft and the figs begin to release their juices. Drizzle with the remaining tablespoon of honey and sprinkle with some more black pepper. Serve either warm or cold.

COOK'S NOTE  If you're not a fan of the grassy pungency of goat cheese, swap it out with a milder ricotta.

# BEER, MEAD, AND CIDER
## FROM THE YAWNING PORTAL
### IN WATERDEEP

Everyone knows the Yawning Portal, at least by reputation. A true adventurer's inn, it takes its name from the threatening dark well at the center of the main floor that offers access to the dungeons of the Undermountain. Many brave souls have ventured into the well on a quest: a smaller number have returned to recuperate in the Yawning Portal's warm and comfortable rooms.

An emboldening tankard of beer, mead, or cider before departure is standard for many adventurers, and many more tankards are enjoyed if they make it back. Some have said that if every drop of beer ever served at the Yawning Portal were to be poured down the well, it would drown the whole of the Undermountain!

# THE YAWNING PORTAL

☐ Beer ☒ Mead ☐ Cider

BREWED AND BOTTLED ON SITE

# SHADOWDARK

During a night of joyous debauchery at the Yawning Portal, it is sometimes easy to forget that unspeakable horror and terrible danger lurk just a stumble away. This frothy concoction called Shadowdark is a reminder of sorts: blood red and stormy, edged with bitterness and a rich cherry sourness. The flesh of mashed cherries swirl in its depths like a promise of devastation, and the final chewy swallow is a moment of sweet release.

If that all sounds a little theatrical, well, you should know that this drink did not come to the Yawning Portal from the dangerous and often brutal worlds of duergar and drow. This drink came from dramatic surface-dwellers, who have a romantic and largely inaccurate conception of the Undermountain as a place of sexy mystery and miserable poetry. It is on the menu at the Yawning Portal because gloomy younger patrons drink a lot of it.

## SERVES 2

| 4 CHERRIES, PITTED | 12 OUNCES EUROPEAN-STYLE LAGER | 12 OUNCES HARD CIDER |
| | | 2 OUNCES CHERRY JUICE |

Using a muddler, pulverize 2 cherries in the bottom of each of two pint glasses. Divide the lager and cider evenly between the two glasses. Top each with 1 ounce of cherry juice. Serve at once.

# PIEGLASS

The Pieglass is an indulgent, dessert-like drink that commemorates the first successful venture into the Undermountain by Durnan the Wanderer and his friend Mirt the Merciless. Durnan and Mirt were young men when they discovered the entrance to the labyrinths beneath Mount Waterdeep created by the mad mage Halaster Blackcloak. They returned from that expedition weighed down with riches, and Durnan's girlfriend, Mhaere, baked a pumpkin pie to celebrate. Mhaere also made Durnan promise that he would stop chasing danger when they had money enough to start a family. In exchange, while his adventures continued, she swore she would always be there to welcome him home with her pie.

Durnan kept his word, and Mhaere kept hers. Together, they built the Yawning Portal over the gateway to the Undermountain. Though Mhaere would not offer just anyone her pie, she did agree to let Durnan add a drink to the menu in her honor.

=== SERVES 2 ===

| PUMPKIN PIE SYRUP | ⅓ CUP WATER | ½ CUP HEAVY CREAM |
|---|---|---|
| 1 TEASPOON PUMPKIN PIE SPICE | ¼ CUP PUMPKIN PUREE | 1 TABLESPOON CONFECTIONERS' SUGAR |
| ½ CUP GRANULATED SUGAR | ½ TEASPOON PURE VANILLA EXTRACT | 24 OUNCES HARD CIDER |
| | | 1 CUP VANILLA ICE CREAM |

*To make the pumpkin pie syrup:* In a small saucepan, cook the pumpkin puree over low heat for about 3 minutes, stirring constantly until thickened and slightly darker in color. Add the pumpkin pie spice, granulated sugar, and water and stir to combine. Increase the heat to medium-high and bring to a simmer, stirring occasionally. Simmer for 2 minutes and remove from the heat. Set a fine-mesh strainer over a heatproof container and pour the syrup through to remove the solids, stirring with a rubber spatula if necessary to drain. Let the syrup cool completely before using. Store any remaining pumpkin pie syrup in an airtight container in the refrigerator for up to 1 week.

In a medium bowl, combine the heavy cream and confectioners' sugar. Using an electric hand mixer or whisk, beat the mixture until soft peaks form. Pour 12 ounces of cider into each of two pint glasses. Add ½ cup of ice cream to each glass, being careful not to overfill. Top each glass with a dollop of whipped cream and drizzle with 2 tablespoons of pumpkin pie syrup. Serve at once.

# BITTER BLACK

For those who return from the Undermountain, a Pieglass may be raised. For those that do not, there is the Bitter Black. This blend of stout, syrup, and dark coffee is as bitter and black as its name and as bitter and black as the mood of those who leave friends or loved ones behind beneath the mountain. There is a cruel uncertainty when no members of an adventuring party return through the portal: Could they still be alive? Have they found some other way out? There is an equally cruel certainty when only some of a party return with news that they saw their friends devoured by spiders, drowned in the Slitherswamp, or torn to pieces by goblin werebats.

There is no dollop of ice cream in a pint glass for the tired and traumatized survivors of such an experience. They have stared into the bitter black, and all they can hope to do is to take strength from it.

---

SERVES 2

24 OUNCES STOUT

2 OUNCES ESPRESSO

1 OUNCE MAPLE SYRUP
(SEE COOK'S NOTE)

---

In each of two pint glasses, pour 12 ounces of stout. Add half of the espresso and maple syrup to each glass and stir gently with a long-handled spoon. Serve at once.

COOK'S NOTE Make sure to use amber or dark amber maple syrup here, if available!

BEER, MEAD, AND CIDER

# CHERRY MEAD

Travelers and adventurers often stop by the Yawning Portal to seek the wisdom of those who have walked the paths before them. A veteran adventurer can sometimes make a steady living just by setting up at a table by the well and waiting for admirers to stop by with a few coins of gold or an offer of a warm meal and a tall drink.

Volo Geddarm, renowned scholar of monsters and magic and author of many guides to the lands and cultures of Faerûn, is one of those veterans at the Yawning Portal. All he asks in exchange for his words of wisdom is that adventurers bring a pitcher of Volo's favorite cherry mead to the table—and something for themselves. Volo is a gregarious and loquacious drinking companion, and he can polish off a whole pitcher in short order, which makes him even more talkative. This sweet and fragrant drink is the lubricant to learn everything you need to from Volo Geddarm. You might bring some coin as well. Volo often has copies of his books for sale just under the table.

SERVES 6 TO 8, OR 1 VOLO GEDDARM

1 (750 ML) BOTTLE
HONEY MEAD

1 CUP CHERRY JUICE

¼ CUP MARASCHINO LIQUEUR

½ TABLESPOON ROSE WATER

1 TEASPOON PURE
VANILLA EXTRACT

ROUGHLY CRACKED OR
SMALL ICE CUBES

In a large pitcher, combine the mead, cherry juice, maraschino liqueur, rose water, and vanilla. Fill the pitcher halfway with ice and stir with a long-handled spoon to combine. Serve at once in rocks or stemless wine glasses.

# TAVERN PUNCH

This refreshing summer punch was designed by Durnan with a very specific customer in mind: the customer who does not want to come inside the Yawning Portal. These people might want to visit and perhaps look inside. They may even take a Yawning Portal beermat to show their friends back home, but the idea of sitting in a room with a giant hole in the middle that leads to near-certain death does not relax them. The possibility of seeing someone emerge from the portal screaming in pain with their arm ripped off or weeping over the death of their best friend does not put them in a drinking mood. And the chance—slim as it is—of a powerful lich lord emerging from the portal in a cloud of death does not sound to them like a fun night out. It takes all sorts to make a city.

For those customers, a table can be set up in front of the tavern in the warm sunshine. They can order a pitcher of this delicious drink and can imagine, just for a moment, what it might be like to live in a world without any dragons.

### SERVES 6 TO 8

| 10 STRAWBERRIES, HULLED AND QUARTERED | 4 CUPS OR 3 (12-OUNCE) BOTTLES LAGER | 1 CUP FRESH BLOOD ORANGE JUICE |
|---|---|---|
| | 3 CUPS GINGER BEER | ½ CUP FRESH LEMON JUICE |

In a large pitcher or punch bowl, muddle the strawberries, completely breaking them down. Add the lager, ginger beer, blood orange juice, and lemon juice and gently stir with a long-handled spoon. Serve at once.

# BEE WELL

The path from the Yawning Portal to the Undermountain is not one only reserved for adventurers. Sometimes things from the Undermountain try to come up, as was the case when a swarm of giant bees buzzed out of the shadows seemingly ready to slaughter the patrons. The patrons drew swords to defend themselves before the halfling druid Blossom Snobeedle stepped forward and calmed both sides of the potential conflict.

Snobeedle, an elder member of the wilderness protectors known as the Emerald Enclave, recognized that the creatures were acting in distress and not anger. By accident or mischief, something had transformed ordinary bees into these daunting giants. Blossom did not have power enough to turn them all back, so she ventured into the Undermountain herself, sought out the queen of the hive, and transformed her back to her normal size. The other bees of the hive magically followed suit, instantly ending the threat to Waterdeep.

Blossom Snobeedle found the bees a new home at the Snobeedle Orchard and Meadery in Undercliff, just beyond the city walls. The mead from the meadery became the key ingredient in a Bee Well, a delicious cocktail that combines the beauty and bounty of nature with a sour sting.

## SERVES 2

| | | |
|---|---|---|
| 1-INCH PIECE FRESH GINGER, PEELED AND THINLY SLICED | 1 OUNCE ORANGE LIQUEUR, SUCH AS COINTREAU | 2 LARGE EGG WHITES |
| 5 OUNCES HONEY MEAD | 1 OUNCE FRESH LEMON JUICE | ROUGHLY CRACKED OR SMALL ICE CUBES |
| | ½ OUNCE HONEY | HONEYCOMB, FOR GARNISH |

In a cocktail shaker, muddle the ginger to release the juices. Add the mead, orange liqueur, lemon juice, honey, and egg whites. Cover and shake for 1 minute to emulsify the egg whites. Remove the lid and fill the cocktail shaker halfway with ice. Cover and shake for 30 seconds until chilled. Strain and divide the mixture between two old-fashioned glasses, making sure to evenly distribute the foam. Garnish with honeycomb and serve at once.

COOK'S NOTE  It's important to shake the ingredients without ice first so that the egg whites can emulsify and give the drink a light and frothy texture. If the liquids are too cold, the egg whites won't fully incorporate.

# ILLUSKAN MULLED CIDER

The tough Northlanders of Luskan have endured many long, bitter winters; some winters have even frozen the wide Mirar River solid and trapped the fine ships that are the heart and engine of the City of Sails.

Illuksan mulled cider is sold on many street corners across the city, often simmering for hours in large iron pots over coal braziers, and the five gangs that dominate the city each have their own preferred vendors and recipes. The folks at Ship Kurth enjoy a fragrant cider with plenty of ginger and cardamom, the Ship Baram gang go heavy on the oranges, and the Ship Suljack folk add more maple syrup to their cider than most people can stand. All five Ships agree that Illuskan mulled cider can only be made from the region's own hardy orchard stock. When word spread that the Yawning Portal proprietor, Durnan, was selling "Illuskan mulled cider" made with Waterdhavian apples, they sent an envoy to advise him of his mistake. The Kurth recipe is now the standard at the Yawning Portal.

## SERVES 6 TO 8

| | | |
|---|---|---|
| 2 CUPS APPLE CIDER | 2 CLOVES | ½ APPLE, SLICED ¼ INCH THICK |
| ¼ CUP MAPLE SYRUP | 2 ALLSPICE BERRIES | ½ ORANGE, SLICED ¼ INCH THICK |
| 1-INCH PIECE FRESH GINGER, PEELED AND THINLY SLICED | 1 TEASPOON CARDAMOM PODS | 1 (750 ML) BOTTLE HARD CIDER |
| 2 CINNAMON STICKS | 1 STAR ANISE | FRESHLY GRATED NUTMEG, FOR GARNISH |

In a medium saucepan, combine the apple cider, maple syrup, ginger, cinnamon sticks, cloves, allspice, cardamom, star anise, apple, orange, and half of the hard cider with a wooden spoon. Set the saucepan over medium-high heat and bring the mixture to a bare simmer. Decrease the heat to low and simmer, covered, for at least 1 and up to 3 hours. The flavors will meld together more the longer you cook. Remove from the heat. Set a fine-mesh strainer over a heatproof bowl and strain the apple cider mixture into it. Add the remaining half of the hard cider and stir to combine. Garnish with nutmeg. Serve at once in mugs or teacups.

COOK'S NOTE Don't allow your hard cider to come to a boil or you'll risk cooking off some of the alcohol content.

# LUIRIC RAREBIT

Rarebit is a simple but delicious tavern treat for hardworking adventurers originating among the halflings of Luiren. Any proud halfling will tell you that they eat and drink very *good* bread, cheese, and beer because "simple" is not the same as "unsophisticated." Delicious rarebit can be made from cheap ingredients and leftover bits of cheese, which is good news for Ogawane Hinkille, the halfling chef at the Yawning Portal, who allegedly makes his rarebit from whatever scraps he can salvage from the tavern floor. (This is not recommended for the home cook.)

### SERVES 4 TO 6

| | | |
|---|---|---|
| 2 TABLESPOONS SALTED BUTTER | ¼ TEASPOON CAYENNE PEPPER | 1 POUND MATURE CHEDDAR CHEESE, GRATED |
| 2 TABLESPOONS ALL-PURPOSE FLOUR | 2 TABLESPOONS WORCESTERSHIRE SAUCE | 4 TO 6 SLICES RYE BREAD, DEPENDING ON SIZE OF LOAF |
| 1 TABLESPOON ENGLISH OR DIJON MUSTARD | ¾ CUP STRONG DARK ALE | 1 TABLESPOON CHOPPED CHIVES |

Preheat the broiler on high with the oven rack set 6 inches from the heating element. Line a baking sheet with foil.

In a medium saucepan, melt the butter over medium heat,. Sprinkle in the flour, stirring constantly until golden brown and nutty, 2 to 3 minutes. Add the mustard, cayenne, and Worcestershire sauce. Stir to combine. Whisk in the dark ale until the mixture is uniform and smooth. Decrease the heat to low and stir in three-quarters of the cheese. Continue to stir until completely smooth. Remove from the heat.

Arrange the bread on the prepared baking sheet and broil until golden brown, about 2 minutes. Remove from the oven and flip the slices over. Spread a thick layer of the cheese sauce onto the untoasted side of the bread and sprinkle the remaining quarter of the cheese evenly over the top. Return the baking sheet to the broiler and cook until the cheese is bubbling and edges of the toast are browned and crisp, 3 to 5 minutes. Slice each piece in half and top with the chives. Serve at once.

# NONALCOHOLIC REFRESHMENTS
FROM **THE HISSING STONES**
IN **BALDUR'S GATE**

The Hissing Stones is a popular public bath house in the Seatower district of Baldur's Gate, renowned for its strictly enforced rules of neutrality. No one comes armed to the Stones, and old grudges are left at the door. The bathhouse is the perfect place for warring factions to negotiate.

The Hissing Stones have a zero-tolerance policy for intoxication, but patrons can enjoy delicious drinks made with bright fresh fruit juices or calming teas. Moon elf owner Merilyn Allaryr says many wars begun over whiskey have ended with peace over peach juice!

# THE HISSING STONES

VITALIZING

NUTRITIOUS

RESTORATIVE

FRESHLY

STEEPED, PRESSED

OR SQUEEZED

## NONALCOHOLIC
## REFRESHMENT

# LATHANDER'S BOUNTY

Lathander the Morninglord, god of the rising sun, the new day, hope, and fresh beginnings, gives his name to this bright and enlivening fruit drink that is the perfect way to start the morning, especially after a grim night.

Golden, handsome, and eternally fresh-faced, Lathander is a favorite god among the athletically inclined. Lathander's bounty is nothing so crass as riches or fame, but the healthy and invigorating natural bounty of fresh bright peaches and sweet sunny mangos that are emblematic of Lathander's radiant aspect. Paladins in service to Lathander will often stop at the Hissing Stones to exercise and take the waters. This is the drink they almost always order. The less athletically inclined also sometimes order it in the desperate hope that it will give them abs and lustrous golden hair. Who knows, maybe one day it will!

### SERVES 2

| | | |
|---|---|---|
| 2 RIPE PEACHES, PITTED AND QUARTERED | ½ CUP PLAIN GREEK YOGURT | 4 ICE CUBES |
| ½ CUP FRESH OR FROZEN MANGO CHUNKS | 6 RASPBERRIES | ½ CUP CLUB SODA OR SPARKLING WATER |
| | 1 TABLESPOON HONEY | EDIBLE FLOWERS, FOR GARNISH |
| | 6 FRESH BASIL LEAVES | |

In a blender, combine the peaches, mango, yogurt, raspberries, and honey. Cover and blend until smooth, scraping down the sides with a rubber spatula as needed. Add 4 basil leaves and ice cubes and blend until smooth. Remove the lid and add the club soda. Stir to combine. Divide the mixture evenly between two highball glasses. Garnish each with a basil leaf and edible flowers. Serve at once.

# KINSHIP SHRUB

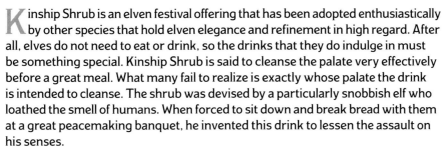

Kinship Shrub is an elven festival offering that has been adopted enthusiastically by other species that hold elven elegance and refinement in high regard. After all, elves do not need to eat or drink, so the drinks that they do indulge in must be something special. Kinship Shrub is said to cleanse the palate very effectively before a great meal. What many fail to realize is exactly whose palate the drink is intended to cleanse. The shrub was devised by a particularly snobbish elf who loathed the smell of humans. When forced to sit down and break bread with them at a great peacemaking banquet, he invented this drink to lessen the assault on his senses.

The drink became popular at such feasts among both elves and humans: Elves shared the creator's delicate sensitivities, and humans thought they were being offered something ceremonial. Of course, it found a place on the menu of the Hissing Stones, where feasts are rare but difficult diplomatic conversations are commonplace.

## SERVES 2

| | | |
|---|---|---|
| 1 LEMON, WASHED AND SLICED INTO ¼-INCH-THICK ROUNDS | ½ CUP SUGAR | 8 OUNCES CLUB SODA |
| 2 SPRIGS FRESH ROSEMARY | ½ CUP APPLE CIDER OR CHAMPAGNE VINEGAR | 2 THINLY SLICED LEMON ROUNDS, FOR GARNISH |
| 1 TEASPOON CUMIN SEEDS | ROUGHLY CRACKED OR SMALL ICE CUBES | 2 SPRIGS FRESH ROSEMARY, FOR GARNISH |

In a wide-mouth jar or lidded pint container, place the lemon, rosemary, and cumin seeds. Add the sugar and stir to combine, lightly mashing the sugar into the fruit. Cover and allow to macerate for 2 hours. Add the vinegar to the jar and stir to combine. Cover and let rest in a cool, dry place for 3 days, shaking daily. Pass the mixture through a fine-mesh strainer to remove the solids and return it to a clean jar. The shrub may be kept in the refrigerator for several months and will improve in flavor over time.

Fill two rocks glasses three-quarters of the way with ice. Add 1¼ ounces of shrub to each glass and top with 4 ounces of club soda. Stir gently to combine. Garnish with lemon rounds and a rosemary sprig. Serve at once.

COOK'S NOTE Shrubs are a great way to add layers of complexity to any cocktail. Once you know the method, they're easy to customize with whatever flavor profile you desire. Stick to the formula of 1 part sugar, 1 part fruit, 1 part vinegar and experiment to your heart's content!

# BALDURIAN TONIC

The great adventurer Minsc the Mighty and his companion animal, Boo, a miniature giant space hamster, are hailed as heroes across the Sword Coast for the many times they saved people from horrifying threats. In recognition of their great deeds, they are gifted food, drink, and other pleasures wherever they go—something that the naïve Minsc assumes is an everyday experience for everyone.

When Minsc came to the Hissing Stones early in the fifteenth century, Merilyn Allaryr gave him the venue's specialty on the house, a restorative Baldurian tonic. Minsc did not get even one sip of the sweet, zesty drink before a cry from the streets called him back into action. He did not return, and within days, Minsc and Boo were lost and feared dead. Merilyn kept Minsc's drink untouched on the bar, and with a touch of magic, the tonic did not lose a single bubble over the ensuing decades. None were allowed to disturb it. Merilyn believed that Minsc would return, and she wanted the drink to be there for him when he did.

Almost seventy years later, the prediction proved true. The petrification spell that had turned Minsc and Boo into statues was finally lifted. Minsc stepped back into the Hissing Stones and found his drink there waiting for him. It is not clear if he knew how long he had been gone.

---

### SERVES 2

| | | |
|---|---|---|
| ½ CUP WATER | ½ CUP SUGAR | 4 OUNCES FRESH LEMON JUICE |
| 2 EARL GREY TEA BAGS | ROUGHLY CRACKED OR SMALL ICE CUBES | 6 OUNCES TONIC WATER |

---

In a small saucepan, bring the water to a boil over high heat. Remove the pan from the heat and immediately add the Earl Grey tea bags. Let steep for 6 minutes, then squeeze the water from the teabags and discard. Add the sugar to the saucepan and stir to combine. Set the saucepan over medium-high heat and bring the mixture to a boil. Reduce the heat to low and simmer for 5 minutes, until slightly thickened. Remove from the heat. Allow the syrup to fully cool before using. Store any remaining Earl Grey syrup in an airtight jar in the refrigerator for up to 1 week.

Fill two highball glasses three-quarters of the way with ice. Add 2 ounces of Earl Grey syrup, 2 ounces lemon juice, and 3 ounces tonic water to each glass. Gently stir to combine. Serve at once.

# MINTWATER

Merilyn Allaryr may well have brought Mintwater to Baldur's Gate and possibly to Faerûn. A moon elf with many centuries of wandering and learning under her belt, Merilyn developed a fondness for mint on her travels and catalogued hundreds of varieties of the herb, noting different properties, uses, and flavors. By some reports, her office at the Stones is lined with jars of dried mint leaves and terrariums of living mint plants, and she has a tome that records many hundreds of recipes for Mintwater.

As far as Merilyn is concerned, there is actually no such thing as Mintwater because it is too simple a name for such a complex idea. Every recipe has its own charms and idiosyncrasies. There was a time when anyone ordering Mintwater at the Stones was met by an overly enthusiastic Merilyn and her giant tome. After several minutes of anguished browsing, patrons would usually order something else or just leave. Merilyn was eventually persuaded to leave the customers alone, and as with every other venue that serves Mintwater, the Stones now offers just one recipe. Unless, of course, you ask to see the book.

=== SERVES 6 TO 8 ===

4 CUPS WATER

½ CUP SUGAR

½ CUP FRESH LIME JUICE

4 PERSIAN CUCUMBERS, ENDS TRIMMED, COARSELY CHOPPED (ABOUT 1 POUND) (SEE COOK'S NOTE)

15 FRESH MINT LEAVES, PLUS MORE FOR GARNISH

ROUGHLY CRACKED OR SMALL ICE CUBES

In a blender jar, blend 2 cups of the water, the sugar, and lime juice for 30 seconds, or until the sugar has dissolved. Add the cucumbers and mint and blend until smooth. Set a fine-mesh strainer over a pitcher and strain the mixture into it, stirring and lightly pressing on the solids if necessary. Add the remaining 2 cups water to the pitcher and stir with a long-handled spoon to combine. Serve in rocks glasses over ice and garnish with extra mint leaves.

COOK'S NOTE Make sure to leave the skins intact on your cucumbers to impart a beautiful green hue on this refreshing drink! Persian cucumbers are thinner skinned, have a lower water content (resulting in more concentrated flavor), and are less astringent than their garden variety cousins. If you can't find them at your local market, English cucumbers will work in their place.

# CHESSENTAN TEA

The people of distant Chessenta have a reputation for intensity. Many great fighters and athletes come from the region, as do many great thinkers and artists. Whatever their calling, Chessentans live life with the fiery passion you might expect of people from a land once ruled by a dragon. In fact, it's home to spellcasters and cultists who would like to see it ruled by a dragon again. Some believe—and some hope—that dragons walk among the people of Chessenta in human form, scheming to reestablish their power.

Hibiscus tea is nearly universally popular in Chessenta, where the hardy flower grows wild in the mountains. A folk tradition emerged of adding hot pepper to the tea when a stranger came to town. If the stranger did not notice the intense heat of the tea, they might be a dragon in disguise.

One cannot be sure that this was ever an effective strategy, as there is no evidence that all dragons share a similar relationship with spice. The point is redundant, however, as people soon developed a taste for increasingly spicy hibiscus tea, and everyone started drinking it that way.

## SERVES 6 TO 8

| JALAPEÑO SYRUP | 4 CUPS WATER | ⅓ CUP FRESH LIME JUICE |
| --- | --- | --- |
| ½ CUP SUGAR | 6 HIBISCUS TEA BAGS | ½ CUP FRESH ORANGE JUICE |
| ½ CUP WATER | ROUGHLY CRACKED OR SMALL ICE CUBES | EDIBLE FLOWERS, TO GARNISH |
| 1 JALAPEÑO, TRIMMED AND SLICED ¼ INCH THICK | | JALAPEÑO SLICES, TO GARNISH |

*To make the jalepeño syrup:* In a small saucepan, bring the water and sugar to a boil over medium-high heat. Add the jalapeños, reduce the heat to low, and simmer for 3 minutes. Remove from the heat and allow the syrup to steep for 10 minutes. Set a fine-mesh strainer over a heatproof container and pour the syrup through to remove the solids. Let cool completely before use and store the jalapeño syrup in the refrigerator for up to 1 week.

In a medium saucepan, bring 2 cups of the water to a boil over high heat. Add the tea bags and let steep for 6 minutes. Remove the tea bags and cool for 5 minutes. Fill a large pitcher three-quarters of the way with ice. Add the brewed tea, remaining 2 cups of water, ⅓ cup of jalapeño syrup, lime juice, and orange juice. Stir with a long-handled spoon to combine. Serve in rocks glasses over ice and garnish with edible flowers and jalapeño slices.

COOK'S NOTE  You can easily customize the heat level of your syrup by adjusting the length of time you steep the jalapeños for. Make sure to taste-test the syrup before adding it to your tea.

# RESTORATION

I n the heat of battle, a spell or potion of restoration can be vital in lifting a
curse, undoing petrification, or just getting someone back on their feet after
a tough bout. When a potion of restoration is hard to find, a pitcher of coconut
water, lemons, and honey can really hit the spot.

Restoration punch was created by a healer exhausted by her reckless
adventuring party's endless demand for potions. She mixed together this
alcohol-free refresher and served it to the party as a "potion of really minor
restoration" with instructions to rest so that the magic could take effect. The
fake potion became a popular trick among healers. Now the drink is a go-to
at places like the Hissing Stones. Most people realize that the potion isn't real—
but they also believe that maybe it might be.

### SERVES 6 TO 8

| | | |
|---|---|---|
| 3 CUPS COCONUT WATER, PREFERABLY PRESSED | 1¼ CUPS FRESH LEMON JUICE | 1 LEMON, SLICED INTO ¼-INCH ROUNDS |
| 1 CUP COCONUT MILK (SEE COOK'S NOTE) | ½ CUP HONEY | ROUGHLY CRACKED OR SMALL ICE CUBES |

In a large pitcher, combine the coconut water, coconut milk, lemon juice,
and honey. Using a long-handled spoon, stir well until the honey is dissolved.
Add the lemon slices. Fill the pitcher halfway with ice and serve in highball
glasses at once.

COOK'S NOTE  Make sure to shake or stir the coconut milk smooth before adding it to the
pitcher. Canned coconut milk tends to separate due to its fat content. It will be easier to
incorporate into the final beverage if it's already homogenous.

# MOURNING CUP

There were two silent monks who lived centuries ago at a temple near Baldur's Gate and they shared a loving bond of devotion as great as any offered to the gods. The story goes that when one of the pair lay on the threshold of death, the other gestured for the reaper to sit and take tea. The monk prepared a syrup of rosemary, the herb of remembrance. He brewed two cups of green tea and set them on the doorstep on a chilly morning to slowly steep and develop flavor. The monk used this time to cherish the last hours of his beloved friend's life and to set firm in his memory all that he loved about him. He and the reaper drank together in quiet contemplation, enjoying the sweetness of honey, the savor of rosemary, and the vivacity of green tea. This drink is now served at the Hissing Stones and always enjoyed in silent remembrance.

## SERVES 2

| | | |
|---|---|---|
| 1 SPRIG FRESH ROSEMARY | 3 CUPS WATER | ROUGHLY CRACKED OR SMALL ICE CUBES |
| 2 GREEN TEA BAGS OR 2 TABLESPOONS LOOSE-LEAF GREEN TEA | 1 TABLESPOON HONEY | |
| | ½ TEASPOON ROSE WATER (OPTIONAL) | |

In a heatproof glass measuring cup, using a muddler, lightly bruise the rosemary to release aroma from the leaves. Add the tea bags to the measuring cup. Set aside.

Into a carafe or small pitcher, pour 2½ cups of water and set aside.

In a small saucepan, bring the remaining ½ cup of water to a boil over high heat. Stir the honey into the boiling water and remove the pan from the heat. Pour the hot water over the rosemary and tea bag. Let sit for 30 seconds and pour the entire contents of the measuring cup into the carafe. Stir to combine. Transfer to the refrigerator and let steep 4 to 8 hours, until your desired strength is reached. Strain and stir in the rose water, if using. Divide between two highball glasses and serve over ice.

COOK'S NOTE This drink utilizes a cold brew method for extracting the tea. While this process does take more time, the results are worth the wait. With some patience, you'll be left with a smooth and balanced tea with less bitterness.

# TEAROOM COOKIES

The Hissing Stones offers a range of relaxation and restoration techniques from various traditions across the continents, from meditation to mud baths. One technique that seems to arise in almost all cultures is enjoying a quiet cup of tea and some cookies.

The legendary kenku monk Whey-Shu brought the recipe for these cookies to Baldur's Gate. Raised in a monastery after goblins destroyed her flock, Whey-Shu devoted her life to the Way of the Shadow, finding strength in silence and power in subtle action. These tearoom cookies are appropriately delicate in texture and flavor. They do not overwhelm the senses.

## MAKES 24 COOKIES

2 CUPS ALL-PURPOSE FLOUR

2½ TABLESPOONS MATCHA POWDER

¼ TEASPOON KOSHER SALT

1 CUP UNSALTED BUTTER, SOFTENED

¾ CUP CONFECTIONERS' SUGAR

1 LARGE EGG YOLK

¼ CUP CHOPPED PISTACHIOS (OPTIONAL)

Set a fine-mesh strainer over a large bowl and sift the flour, matcha powder, and salt into it.

In the bowl of a stand mixer fitted with the paddle attachment, beat the butter on medium speed until soft. Scrape down the sides of the bowl. Add the confectioners' sugar and beat on medium speed until fluffy and pale yellow, 1 to 2 minutes. Add the egg yolk and beat until incorporated. Reduce the speed to low, add in the flour mixture, and beat until just incorporated, making sure to scrape down the sides if needed. Turn the dough out onto a countertop lined with plastic wrap and shape it into a neat log 1 to 1½ inches in diameter and 12 inches long. Wrap the dough in plastic wrap and refrigerate for at least 2 hours and up to 1 week, until well chilled.

Preheat the oven to 350°F. Line two baking sheets with parchment paper.

Unwrap the dough and slice it into ⅓-inch-thick rounds. Arrange the cookie dough on the prepared baking sheets, leaving at least 1 inch of space between the cookies. Sprinkle the chopped pistachios on each cookie. Bake, one tray at a time (keep the other tray chilled in the refrigerator), for 11 to 13 minutes, until the cookies are set and the edges are slightly golden. Cool on the baking sheet for 5 minutes before transferring to a wire rack.

# ACKNOWLEDGMENTS

Thank you to the Danger Dice Gang—Jim, Stacy, Tory, Kean, and Derek—for being the best dang adventure party to drink with. Thank you to the Lady Snakes—Levi, Grant, Carl, Jomar, Shane, and Matty—for indulging my hosting excesses. Thank you to Chris and Andrew for enriching my bar, and thank you all for enriching my life!

## ABOUT THE AUTHOR

Andrew Wheeler is a fantasy author and food writer based in Toronto, Ontario. He is coauthor of the Dungeons & Dragons Young Adventurer's Guide series, bringing D&D to the juice box crowd, and the cocreator of the comics *Sins of the Black Flamingo*, *Cat Fight*, *Love and War*, and *Hey, Mary*. He lives with a rescue named Barb, a glass-fronted antique console drinks cabinet that he saved from the trash.

# INDEX

Note: Page references in *italics* indicate photographs.

189

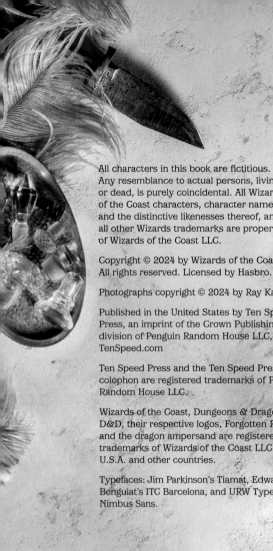

Published in the United States by Ten Speed Press, an imprint of the Crown Publishing Group, a division of Penguin Random House LLC, New York. TenSpeed.com

Typefaces: Jim Parkinson's Tiamat, Edward Benguiat's ITC Barcelona, and URW Type Foundry's Nimbus Sans.

Library of Congress Cataloging-in-Publication Data

Names: Wheeler, Andrew, 1976- author. | Stoyanov, Ashley, writer of supplementary textual content. | Kachatorian, Ray, photographer. Title: Puncheons & flagons : the official Dungeons & Dragons cocktail book / Andrew Wheeler ; recipes by Ashley Stoyanov ; photographs by Ray Kachatorian. Other titles: Puncheons and flagons. Identifiers: LCCN 2023040054 (print) | LCCN 2023040055 (ebook) | ISBN 9781984862525 (hardcover) | ISBN 9781984862532 (ebook) Subjects: LCSH: Cocktails. | Dungeons and Dragons (Game) | Literary cookbooks. lcgft Classification: LCC TX951 .W444 2024 (print) | LCC TX951 (ebook) | DDC 641.87/4--dc23/eng/20230926
LC record available at https://lccn.loc.gov/2023040054
LC ebook record available at https://lccn.loc.gov/2023040055

Hardcover ISBN: 978-1-9848-6252-5
eBook ISBN: 978-1-9848-6253-2

Printed in China

Acquiring editor: Shaida Boroumand
Project editor: Claire Yee
Production editor: Natalie Blachere
Designer: Kelly Booth
Art directors: Kelly Booth and Emma Campion
Production designers: Mari Gill and Faith Hague
Production manager: Serena Sigona
Prepress color manager: Jane Chinn
Photo retouchers: Tamara White, Kelly Booth, and Claudia Sanchez
Photo assistant: Jeff Johnson
Food stylist: Amanda Anselmino
Food stylist assistant: Huxley McCorkle
Prop stylist: Glenn Jenkins
Prop stylist assistant: Zach Wine
Copyeditor: Hope Clarke | Proofreader: Mike Richards | Indexer: Ken DellaPenta
Publicist: Maya Bradford | Marketer: Paola Crespo

Wizards of the Coast team: Paul Morrissey

Scene Illustrations: Goodname Digital Art Studio
Labels and motifs: Widakk Design
Photomontage: Kelly Booth, incorporating select background elements courtesy of Adobe Stock and map art by Jared Blando

10 9 8 7 6 5 4 3 2 1

First Edition